AA

PHRASE BOOK

Spanish

English edition prepared by First Edition Translations Ltd, Great Britain
Designed and produced by AA Publishing
First published in 1995 as Wat & Hoe Portugees,

A CIP catalogue record for this book is available from the British Library
Published by AA Publishing (a trading name of Automobile Association Developments Limited, whose registered office is Fanum House, Basingstoke, Hampshire RG21 4EA.
Registered number 1878835)

A02536

Typeset by Information Engineers, Cambridge.
Printed and bound by Everbest Printing Co Ltd, China.
Find out more about AA Publishing and the wide range of services the AA provides by visiting our web site at
www.theAA.com/bookshop

Contents

Contents

Introduction

● **Welcome to the AA's essential Phrase Books series**, covering the most popular European languages and containing everything you'd expect from a comprehensive language series. They're concise, accessible and easy to understand, and you'll find them indispensable on your trip abroad.

Each guide is divided into 15 themed sections and starts with a pronunciation table which gives you the phonetic spelling to all the words and phrases you'll need to know for your trip, while at the back of the book is an extensive word list and grammar guide which will help you construct basic sentences in your chosen language.

Throughout the book you'll come across coloured boxes with a ☞ beside them. These are designed to help you if you can't understand what your listener is saying to you. Hand the book over to them and encourage them to point to the appropriate answer to the question you are asking.

Other coloured boxes in the book - this time without the symbol - give alphabetical listings of themed words with their English translations beside them.

For extra clarity, we have put all English words and phrases in black, foreign language terms in red and their phonetic pronunciation in italic.

This phrase book covers all subjects you are likely to come across during the course of your visit, from reserving a room for the night to ordering food and drink at a restaurant and what to do if your car breaks down or you lose your traveller's cheques and money. With over 2,000 commonly used words and essential phrases at your fingertips you can rest assured that you will be able to get by in all situations, so let the essential Phrase Book become your passport to a secure and enjoyable trip!

Pronunciation table

The pronunciation provided should be read as if it were English, bearing in mind the following main points:

Vowels

Vowels in Spanish are very open

a	is like **a** in **a**mber,	***ah***	as in **casa**	*kahsah*
e	is like **e** in **e**gg,	***eh***	as in **esta**	*ehstah*
i	is like **ee** in s**ee**n,	***ee***	as in **isla**	*eeslah*
o	is like **o** in J**o**hn,	***oh***	as in **hotel**	*ohtehl*
u	is like **oo** in r**oo**m,	***oo***	as in **uno**	*oonoh*
y	is like **ee** in s**ee**n,	***ee***	as in **y**	*ee*
	the diphthong **ay** is pronounced as in aisle or eye		as in **hay**	*eye*

Consonants

Consonants are as in English, pronounced less clearly, except

b/v	are pronounced roughly the same	as in **vamos**	*bahmohs*
c	before e and i is soft and is like the **th** in **th**atch	as in **la acera**	*lah ahthehrah*
	before a,o and u is hard	as in **cosa**	*kohsah*
cu	before another vowel is pronounced like **cw**	as in **la cuenta**	*lah kwehntah*
g	before e and i is soft and is like the Scottish **ch** in lo**ch**,	as in **la gente**	*lah hehnteh*
	before a, o and u is hard	as in **gato**	*ghahtoh*
gu	before e and i is pronounced as hard **g**	as in **la guía**	*geeah*
	before a, o and u is pronounced like **gw**	as in **guapo**	*gwahpoh*

gü	before e and i is pronounced like **gw**		
		as in **lingüística**	*leengweesteekah*
h	is silent		
j	is like the soft **g**	as in **jarra**	*hahrrah*
ll	is like **lli** in bi**ll**ion	as in **llave**	*lyahbeh*
ñ	is like **ni** in o**ni**on	as in **año**	*ahnyoh*
r	is rolled as in the Scottish **r**, **rr** is a longer roll		
z	is like **th** in **th**ought	as in **taza**	*tahthah*

The stress normally falls on the last syllable of the word (**hotel**), except that words ending in a vowel (not including **y**) or in n or s (**casa**, **casas**) are stressed on the next to the last syllable. All exceptions are indicated by a written acute accent (**Córdoba**, *kohrdohbah*).

Note: In the south, the soft **c** and the **z** are pronounced **s**. This is also true in Latin America.

1 Useful lists

1.1 Today or tomorrow?

What day is it today?	¿Qué día es hoy? *keh deeah ehs oy?*
Today's Monday	Hoy es lunes *oy ehs loonehs*
– Tuesday	Hoy es martes *oy ehs mahrtehs*
– Wednesday	Hoy es miércoles *oy ehs myehrkohlehs*
– Thursday	Hoy es jueves *oy ehs hooehbehs*
– Friday	Hoy es viernes *oy ehs byehrnehs*
– Saturday	Hoy es sábado *oy ehs sahbahdoh*
– Sunday	Hoy es domingo *oy ehs dohmeengoh*
in January	en enero *ehn ehnehroh*
since February	desde febrero *dehsdeh fehbrehroh*
in spring	en primavera *ehn preemahbehrah*
in summer	en verano *ehn behrahnoh*
in autumn	en otoño *ehn ohtohnyoh*
in winter	en invierno *ehn eenbyehrno*
1997	mil novecientos noventa y siete *meel nohbehthyentohs nohbehntah ee syehteh*
the twentieth century	el siglo XX (veinte) *ehl seegloh beheenteh*

What's the date today? ¿Qué día es hoy?
keh deeah ehs oy?

Today's the 24th Hoy es 24 (veinticuatro)
oy ehs beheenteekwahtroh

Monday 3 November 1998 lunes 3 (tres) de noviembre de 1998 (mil novecientos noventa y ocho)
loonehs trehs deh nohbyehmbreh deh meel nohbehthyehntohs nohbehntah ee ohchoh

in the morning por la mañana
pohr lah mahnyahnah

in the afternoon por la tarde
pohr lah tahrdeh

in the evening por la noche
pohr lah nohcheh

at night por la noche
pohr lah nohcheh

this morning esta mañana
ehstah mahnyahnah

this afternoon esta tarde
ehstah tahrdeh

this evening esta noche
ehstah nohcheh

tonight esta noche
ehstah nohcheh

last night anoche
ahnohcheh

this week esta semana
ehstah sehmahnah

next month el mes próximo
ehl mehs prohxeemoh

last year el año pasado
ehl ahnyo pahsahdoh

next... el/la... próximo/a
ehl/lah... prohxeemoh/ah

in...days/weeks/ months/years	dentro de...días/semanas/meses/años *dehntroh deh... deeahs/sehmahnahs/mehsehs/ahnyohs*
...weeks ago	hace...semanas *ahthe...sehmahnahs*
day off	día libre *deeah leebreh*

1.2 Bank holidays

- **The most important** Bank Holidays in Spain are the following:

January 1	New Year's Day (Año Nuevo)
January 6	Epiphany (Epifanía)
March 19	St. Joseph's Day (San José)
March/April	Good Friday (Viernes Santo)
March/April	Easter Monday(Catalonia) (Lunes Santo)
May 1	Labour Day (Día del Trabajo)
May/June	Corpus Christi (Corpus Christi)
July 25	St. James's Day (Santiago)
August 15	Assumption Day (Asunción)
October 12	Columbus Day (Día de las Américas)
November 1	All Saints' Day (Todos los Santos)
December 6	Constitution Day (Día de la Constitución)
December 8	Immaculate Conception (Inmaculada Concepción)
December 25	Christmas (Navidad)

There are also various regional holidays like San Fermín in Pamplona (July 6–13) and the Fallas in Valencia (March 19).

1.3 What time is it?

What time is it?	¿Qué hora es? *keh ohrah ehs?*

It's nine o'clock	Son las nueve *sohn lahs nwehbeh*
– five past ten	Son las diez y cinco *sohn lahs dyeth ee theenkoh*
– a quarter past eleven	Son las once y cuarto *sohn lahs ohntheh ee kwahrtoh*
– twenty past twelve	Son las doce y veinte *sohn lahs dohthe ee beheenteh*
– half past one	Es la una y media *ehs lah oonah ee mehdyah*
– twenty–five to three	Son las tres menos veinticinco *sohn lahs trehs mehnohs beheenteetheenkoh*
– a quarter to four	Son las cuatro menos cuarto *sohn lahs kwahtroh mehnohs kwahrtoh*
– ten to five	Son las cinco menos diez *sohn lahs theenkoh mehnohs dyehth*
– twelve noon	Son las doce del mediodía *sohn lahs dohtheh dehl mehdyohdeeah*
– midnight	Son las doce de la noche *sohn lahs dohtheh deh lah nohcheh*
half an hour	media hora *mehdyah ohrah*
What time?	¿A qué hora? *ah keh ohrah?*
What time can I come round?	¿A qué hora puedo pasar? *ah keh ohrah pwehdoh pahsahr?*
At...	A las... *ah lahs...*
After...	Después de las... *dehspwehs deh lahs...*
Before...	Antes de las... *ahntehs deh lahs...*
Between...and...	Entre las...y las... *ehntreh lahs...ee lahs...*
From...to...	De las...a las... *deh lahs...ah lahs...*

In...minutes	Dentro de...minutos *dehntroh deh...meenootohs*
– an hour	Dentro de una hora *dehntroh deh oonah ohrah*
– ...hours	Dentro de...horas *dehntroh deh...ohrahs*
– a quarter of an hour	Dentro de un cuarto de hora *dehntroh deh oon kwahrtoh deh ohrah*
– three quarters of an hour	Dentro de tres cuartos de hora *dehntroh deh trehs kwahrtohs deh ohrah*
early/late	muy temprano/tarde *mwee tehmprahnoh/tahrdeh*
on time	a tiempo *ah tyehmpoh*
summer opening hours	horario de verano *ohrahryoh deh behrahnoh*
winter opening hours	horario de invierno *ohrahryoh deh eenbyehrnoh*

1.4 One, two, three...

0	cero	*thehroh*
1	uno	*oonoh*
2	dos	*dohs*
3	tres	*trehs*
4	cuatro	*kwahtroh*
5	cinco	*theenkoh*
6	seis	*sehees*
7	siete	*syehteh*
8	ocho	*ohchoh*
9	nueve	*nwehbeh*
10	diez	*dyeth*
11	once	*ohntheh*
12	doce	*dohtheh*
13	trece	*trehtheh*

14 ________________	catorce	*kahtohrtheh*
15 ________________	quince	*keentheh*
16 ________________	dieciséis	*dyetheesehees*
17 ________________	diecisiete	*dyetheesyehteh*
18 ________________	dieciocho	*dyetheeohchoh*
19 ________________	diecinueve	*dyetheenwehbe*
20 ________________	veinte	*beheenteh*
21 ________________	veintiuno	*beheenteeoonoh*
22 ________________	veintidós	*beheenteheedohs*
30 ________________	treinta	*treheentah*
31 ________________	treinta y uno	*treheentah ee oonoh*
32 ________________	treinta y dos	*treheentah ee dohs*
40 ________________	cuarenta	*kwahrehntah*
50 ________________	cincuenta	*theenkwehntah*
60 ________________	sesenta	*sehsehntah*
70 ________________	setenta	*sehtehntah*
80 ________________	ochenta	*ohchehntah*
90 ________________	noventa	*nohvehntah*
100 ________________	cien	*thyehn*
101 ________________	ciento uno	*thyehntoh oonoh*
110 ________________	ciento diez	*thyehntoh dyeth*
120 ________________	ciento veinte	*thyehntoh beheenteh*
200 ________________	doscientos	*dohsthyehntohs*
300 ________________	trescientos	*trehsthyehntohs*
400 ________________	cuatrocientos	*kwahtrohthyehntohs*
500 ________________	quinientos	*keenyehntohs*
600 ________________	seiscientos	*seheesthyehntohs*
700 ________________	setecientos	*sehtehthyehntohs*
800 ________________	ochocientos	*ohchohthyehntohs*
900 ________________	novecientos	*nohbehthyentohs*
1000 ________________	mil	*meel*
1100 ________________	mil cien	*meel thyehn*
2000 ________________	dos mil	*dohs meel*
10,000 ________________	diez mil	*dyeth meel*
100,000 ________________	cien mil	*thyehn meel*
1,000,000________________	un millón	*oon meelyohn*
1st________________	primero	*preemehroh*

2nd ________________	segundo	*sehgoondoh*
3rd ________________	tercero	*tehrthehroh*
4th ________________	cuarto	*kwahrtoh*
5th ________________	quinto	*keentoh*
6th ________________	sexto	*sehxtoh*
7th ________________	séptimo	*sehpteemoh*
8th ________________	octavo	*ohktahboh*
9th ________________	noveno	*nohvehnoh*
10th ________________	décimo	*dehtheemoh*
11th ________________	undécimo	*oondehtheemoh*
12th ________________	duodécimo	*doo-ohdehtheemo*
13th ________________	decimotercero	*dehtheemohtehrthehroh*
14th ________________	decimocuarto	*dehtheemohkwahrtoh*
15th ________________	decimoquinto	*dehtheemohkeentoh*
16th ________________	decimosexto	*dehtheemohsehxtoh*
17th ________________	decimoséptimo	*dehtheemosehpteemoh*
18th ________________	decimoctavo	*dehtheemohktahboh*
19th ________________	decimonoveno	*dehtheemonobenoh*
20th ________________	vigésimo	*beeheseemoh*
21st ________________	vigesimo -primero	*beeheseemohpreemeroh*
22nd ________________	vigesimose -gundo	*beeheseemohsegoondoh*
30th ________________	trigésimo	*treeheseemoh*
100th ________________	centésimo	*thentehseemoh*
1,000th ________________	milésimo	*meelehseemoh*
once ________________	una vez	*oonah behth*
twice ________________	dos veces	*dos behthes*
double ________________	el doble	*ehl dohbleh*
triple ________________	el triple	*ehl treepleh*
half ________________	la mitad	*lah meetath*
a quarter ________________	un cuarto	*oon kwartoh*
a third ________________	un tercio	*oon terthyoh*
a couple, a few, some __	unos, algunos	*oonohs, algoonohs*
2 + 4 = 6 ________________	dos más cuatro, seis	*dohs mahs kwahtroh, sehees*

4 − 2 = 2 ___________	cuatro menos dos, dos *kwahtroh mehnohs dohs, dohs*
2 x 4 = 8 ___________	dos por cuatro, ocho *dohs pohr kwahtroh, ohchoh*
4 ÷ 2 = 2 ___________	cuatro dividido dos, dos *kwahtroh deebeedeedoh dohs, dohs*
odd/even ___________	par/impar *pahr/eempahr*
total ___________	(en) total *(ehn) tohtahl*
6 x 9 ___________	seis por nueve *sehees pohr nwehbeh*

1.5 The weather

Is the weather going to be good/bad? ___	¿Hará buen/mal tiempo? *ahrah bwehn/mahl tyehmpoh?*
Is it going to get colder/hotter? ______	¿Hará más frío/calor? *ahrah mahs freeoh/kahlohr?*
What temperature is it going to be? __	¿Cuántos grados hará? *kwahntohs grahdohs ahrah?*
Is it going to rain? _____	¿Va a llover? *bah ah lyohbehr?*
Is there going to be a storm? __	¿Tendremos tormenta? *tehndrehmohs tohrmehntah?*
Is it going to snow? ____	¿Va a nevar? *bah ah nehbahr?*
Is it going to freeze? ___	¿Va a helar? *bah ah ehlahr?*
Is the thaw setting in? __	¿Comenzará el deshielo? *kohmehnzahrah ehl dehsyeloh*
Is it going to be foggy? _	¿Habrá niebla? *ahbrah nyehblah?*
Is there going to be a thunderstorm? __	¿Habrá tormenta eléctrica? *ahbrah tohrmehntah ehlehktreekah?*

algo
nublado/nublado
light/heavy clouds
bochornoso
stormy
bueno
fine
caluroso
hot
chubasco
shower
cielo cubierto
overcast
desapacible
bleak
despejado
clear
escarcha
frost
fresco
chilly
frìo
cold

granizo
hail
...grados(bajo/sobre cero)
...degrees(above/ below zero)
helada
(black) ice
húmedo
damp
huracán
hurricane
llovizna
drizzle
lluvia
rain
lluvioso
wet
niebla
fog
nieve
snow
nublado
cloudy

ola de calor
heat wave
pesado
muggy
sofocante
scorching hot
soleado
sunny
suave
mild
tormenta eléctrica
thunderstorm
vendaval
gale
ventoso
windy
viento
wind
viento leve /moderado/ fuerte
light/moderate/ strong wind
tempestad
squall

The weather's changing	Va a cambiar el tiempo *bah ah kahmbyahr ehl tyehmpoh*
It's cooling down	Va a refrescar *bah ah rehfrehskahr*
What's the weather going to be like today/ tomorrow?	¿Qué tiempo hará hoy/mañana? *keh tyehmpoh ahrah oy/mahnyahnah?*

1.6 Here, there...

See also 5.1 Asking for directions

here/there	aquí/allá *ahkee/ahlyah*
somewhere/nowhere	en alguna/ninguna parte *ehn algoonah/neengoonah pahrteh*
everywhere	en todas partes *ehn tohdahs pahrtehs*
far away/nearby	lejos/cerca *lehhos/thehrkah*
right/left	a la derecha/izquierda *ah lah dehrehchah/eethkyehrdah*
to the right/left of	a la derecha/izquierda de *ah lah dehrehchah/eethkyehrdah deh*
straight ahead	todo recto *tohdoh rehktoh*
via	pasando por *pahsahndoh pohr*
in	en *ehn*
on	sobre *sohbreh*
under	debajo de *dehbahhoh deh*
against	contra *kohntrah*
opposite	frente a *frehnteh ah*
next to	al lado de *ahl lahdoh deh*
near	junto a *hoontoh ah*
in front of	delante de *dehlahnteh deh*

in the centre ________ en el medio
ehn ehl mehdyoh

forward ________ hacia adelante
ahthyah ahdehlanteh

down ________ (hacia) abajo
(ahthyah) ahbahhoh

up ________ (hacia) arriba
(ahthya) ahrreebah

inside ________ (hacia) adentro
(ahthya) ahdehntroh

outside ________ (hacia) afuera
(ahthya) ahfwehrah

behind ________ (hacia) atrás
(ahthya) ahtrahs

at the front ________ delante
dehlahnteh

at the back ________ detrás
dehtrahs

in the north ________ en el norte
ehn ehl nohrteh

to the south ________ hacia el sur
ahthya ehl soor

from the west ________ del oeste
dehl ohehsteh

from the east ________ del este
dehl ehsteh

...of ________ al...de
ahl...deh

1.7 What does that sign say?

See also 5.4 Traffic signs

abierto/cerrado
open/closed
agua no potable
no drinking water
alta tensión
high voltage
ascensor lift
caballeros
gents/gentlemen
caja pay here
completo full
coto privado
private (property)
cuidado con el perro
beware of the dog
cuidado, escalón
mind the step
entrada
entrance
entrada libre
free admission
escalera stairs
escalera de incendios
fire escape
escalera mecánica
escalator
freno de emergencia
emergency brake
horario (de apertura)
opening hours
información
information
liquidación (por cese)
closing-down sale
no funciona
out of order
no tocar
please do not touch
peligro
danger
peligro de incendio
fire hazard
...piso ...floor
primeros auxilios
first aid
prohibido el paso
no entry
prohibido fotografiar
no photographs
prohibido fumar
no smoking
prohibido hacer fuego
no open fires
prohibido para animales
no pets allowed
prohibido pisar el césped
keep off the grass
razón aquí
inquiries
rebajas
clearance
recepción
reception
recién pintado
wet paint
reservado
reserved
saldos
sale
salida
exit
salida de emergencia/salida de socorro
emergency exit
se alquila
for hire
se ruega no molestar
do not disturb
se vende
for sale
señoras
ladies
servicios
toilets
empujar/tirar
push/pull

1.8 Telephone alphabet

a	*ah*	de Antonio	*deh ahntohnyoh*
b	*beh*	de Barcelona	*deh bahr-thehlohnah*
c	*theh*	de Carmen	*deh kahrmehn*
ch	*cheh*	de chocolate	*deh chohkohlahteh*
d	*deh*	de Dolores	*deh dohlohrehs*
e	*eh*	de Enrique	*deh ehnreekeh*
f	*hefeh*	de Francia	*deh frahnthyah*
g	*heh*	de Gerona	*de hehrohnah*
h	*ahcheh*	de historia	*de eestohryah*
I	*ee*	de Inés	*deh eenehs*
j	*hohtah*	de José	*deh hohseh*
k	*kah*	de Kilo	*deh keeloh*
l	*ehleh*	de Lorenzo	*deh lohrehnthoh*
ll	*ehlyeh*	de Llobregat	*deh lyohbrehgaht*
m	*ehmeh*	de Madrid	*deh Mahdreedh*
n	*ehneh*	de Navarra	*deh nahbahrrah*
ñ	*ehnyeh*	de ñoño	*deh nyohnyoh*
o	*oh*	de Oviedo	*deh ohbyedoh*
p	*peh*	de París	*deh pahrees*
q	*koo*	de querido	*deh kehreedoh*
r	*ehrreh*	de Ramón	*deh rahmohn*
s	*ehseh*	de sábado	*deh sahbahdoh*
t	*teh*	de Tarragona	*deh tahrrahgohnah*
u	*oo*	de Ulises	*deh ooleesehs*
v	*oobeh*	de Valencia	*deh bahlehnthyah*
w	*oobehdohbleh*	de Washington	*deh wahsheengtohn*
x	*ehkees*	de Xiquena	*deh heekehnah*
y	*eegryehgah*	griega	*gryehgah*
z	*thehtah*	de Zaragoza	*deh thahrahgohthah*

1.9 Personal details

surname ______	apellidos	*ahpehlyeedohs*
christian name(s) ______	nombre	*nohmbreh*
initials ______	iniciales	*eeneethyahlehs*
address (street/ number) ______	dirección (calle/número)	*deerehkthyohn (kahlyeh/noomehroh)*
post code/town ______	código postal/población	*cohdeegoh pohstahl/pohblahthyon)*
sex (male/female) ______	sexo (v = varón, m = mujer)	*sehksoh (v = bahrohn, m = moohehr)*
nationality ______	nacionalidad	*nahthyohnahleedahdh*
date of birth ______	fecha de nacimiento	*fehchah deh nahtheemyehntoh*
place of birth ______	lugar de nacimiento	*loogahr deh natheemyehntoh*
occupation ______	profesión	*profehsyohn*
married/single/ divorced ______	casado, casada/soltero, soltera/ divorciado, divorciada	*kahsahdoh, kahsahdah/sohltehroh, sohltehrah/deebohrthyahdoh, deebohrthyahdah*
widowed ______	viuda/viudo	*byoodah/byoodoh*
(number of) children ______	(número de) hijos	*(noomehroh deh) eehohs*
passport/identity card/driving licence/ number, place and date of issue ______	pasaporte/carnet de identidad/permiso de conducir/número, lugar y fecha de expedición	*kahrneh deh eedehnteedahdh (pahsahpohrteh/pehrmeesoh deh kohndootheer) noomehroh, loogahr ee fehchah deh ehkspehdeethyohn*

2

Courtesies

● **Female friends and relatives** kiss on both cheeks in Spain. In shops, etc., you will hear *¡Buenos días!* or just *¡Buenas!*, and expect to be addressed in Basque or Catalan in these provinces. For example you will hear *¡Agur!* instead of *¡Adiós!* in the Basque Country.

2.1 Greetings

Hello, Mr Smith	Hola, buenos días *ohlah, bwehnohs deeahs*
Hello, Peter	Hola, Pedro *ohlah, pehdroh*
Hi, Helen	Qué hay, Elena *keh ay, ehlehnah*
Good morning, madam	Buenos días, señora (before 2pm) *bwehnohs deeahs, sehnyohrah*
Good afternoon, sir	Buenas tardes, señor (after 2pm) *bwehnahs tahrdehs, sehnyohr*
Good evening	Buenas tardes (before 9pm), buenas noches (after 9pm) *bwehnahs tahrdehs, bwehnahs nohchehs*
How are you?	¿Qué tal? *keh tahl?*
Fine, thank you, and you?	Muy bien, ¿y usted? *mwee byehn, ee oostehdh?*
Very well	Estupendo *ehstoopehndoh*
Not very well	Regular *rehgoolahr*
Not too bad	Tirando *teerando*
I'd better be going	Bueno, me voy *bwehnoh, meh boy*
I have to be going. Someone's waiting for me	Tengo que irme. Me están esperando *tehngoh keh eermeh, meh ehstahn ehspehrahndoh*

Bye!	¡Adiós! *ahdyohs!*
Goodbye	Hasta luego *ahstah lwehgoh*
See you soon	Hasta pronto *ahstah prohntoh*
See you later	Hasta luego *ahstah lwehgoh*
See you in a little while	Hasta ahora *ahstah ahohrah*
Sleep well	Que descanse *keh dehskahnseh*
Good night	Buenas noches *bwehnahs nohchehs*
All the best	Que le vaya bien *keh leh bahyah byehn*
Have fun	Que se divierta, que lo pase bien *keh seh deebyehrtah, keh loh pahseh byehn*
Good luck	Mucha suerte *moochah swehrteh*
Have a nice holiday	Felices vacaciones *fehleethehs bahkahthyohnehs*
Have a good trip	Buen viaje *bwehn byahheh*
Thank you, you too	Gracias, igualmente *grahthyahs, eegwahlmehnteh*
Say hello to...for me	Recuerdos a... *rehkwehrdohs ah...*

2.2 How to ask a question

Who?	¿Quién? *kyehn?*
Who's that?	¿Quién es? *kyehn ehs?*

What? ______ ¿Qué?
keh?

What's there to see here? ______ ¿Qué se puede visitar aquí?
keh seh pwehdeh beeseetahr ahkee?

What kind of hotel is that? ______ ¿Qué clase de hotel es?
keh klahseh deh ohtehl ehs?

Where? ______ ¿Dónde?
dohndeh?

Where's the toilet? ______ ¿Dónde están los servicios?
dohndeh ehstahn lohs sehrbeethyohs?

Where are you going? ______ ¿A dónde va?
ahdohndeh bah?

Where are you from? ______ ¿De dónde es usted?
deh dohndeh ehs oostehdh?

How? ______ ¿Cómo?
kohmoh?

How far is that? ______ ¿A qué distancia queda?
ah keh deestahnthyah kehdah?

How long does it take? ______ ¿Cuánto dura?
kwahntoh doorah?

How long is the trip? ______ ¿Cuánto dura el viaje?
kwahntoh doorah ehl byahheh?

How much? ______ ¿Cuánto?
kwahntoh?

How much is this? ______ ¿Cuánto vale?
kwahntoh bahleh?

What time is it? ______ ¿Qué hora es?
keh ohrah ehs?

Which? ______ ¿Cuál? ¿Cuáles?
kwahl? kwahlehs?

Which glass is mine? ______ ¿Cuál es mi copa?
kwahl ehs mee kohpah?

When? ______ ¿Cuándo?
kwahndoh?

When are you leaving? ______ ¿Cuándo sale?
kwahndoh sahleh?

Why?	¿Por qué? *pohr keh?*
Could you...me?	¿Podría...? *pohdreeah...?*
Could you help me, please?	¿Podría ayudarme? *pohdreeah ahyoodahrmeh?*
Could you point that out to me?	¿Me lo podría indicar? *meh loh pohdreeah eendeekahr?*
Could you come with me, please?	¿Le importaría acompañarme? *leh eempohrtahreeah ahkohmpahnyahrmeh?*
Could you...	¿Quiere...?/¿Podría...? *kyehreh...?/pohdreeah...?*
Could you reserve some tickets for me, please?	¿Me podría reservar entradas? *meh pohdreeah rehsehrbahr ehntrahdahs?*
Do you know...?	¿Sabe...? *sahbeh...?*
Do you know another hotel, please?	¿Sabría indicarme otro hotel? *sahbreeah eendeekahrmeh ohtroh ohtehl?*
Do you know whether...?	¿Tiene...? *tyehneh...?*
Do you have a...?	¿Me podría dar un(a)...? *meh pohdreeah dahr oon(ah)...?*
Do you have a vegetarian dish, please?	¿Tendría un plato sin carne? *tehndreeah oon plahtoh seen kahrneh?*
I'd like...	Quisiera... *keesyehrah...*
I'd like a kilo of apples, please.	Quisiera un kilo de manzanas *keesyehrah oon keeloh deh mahnthahnahs*
Can I...?	¿Puedo...?/¿Se puede...? *pwehdoh...?/seh pwehdeh?*
Can I take this?	¿Podría llevármelo? *pohdreeah lyehbahrmehloh?*
Can I smoke here?	¿Se puede fumar aquí? *seh pwehdeh foomahr ahkee?*
Could I ask you something?	¿Puedo hacerle una pregunta? *pwehdoh ahthehrleh oonah prehgoontah?*

2.3 How to reply

Yes, of course	Sí, claro *see, klahroh*
No, I'm sorry	No, lo siento *noh, loh syehntoh*
Yes, what can I do for you?	Sí. ¿En qué puedo servirle? *see, ehn keh pwehdoh sehrbeerleh?*
Just a moment, please	Un momento, por favor *oon mohmehntoh, pohr fahbohr*
No, I don't have time now	No, ahora no tengo tiempo *noh, aohrah noh tehngoh tyehmpoh*
No, that's impossible	No, eso es imposible *noh, ehsoh ehs eempohseebleh*
I think so	Creo que sí *krehoh keh see*
I agree	Yo también lo creo *yoh tahmbyehn loh krehoh*
I hope so too	Yo también lo espero *yoh tahmbyehn loh ehspehroh*
No, not at all	No, de ninguna manera *noh, deh neengoonah mahnehrah*
No, no-one	No, nadie *noh, nahdyeh*
No, nothing	No, nada *noh, nahdah*
That's (not) right	(No) es cierto *(noh) ehs thyehrtoh*
I (don't) agree	(No) estoy de acuerdo con usted *(noh) ehstoy deh ahkwehrdoh kohn oostehdh*
All right	Está bien *ehstah byehn*
Okay	Vale *bahleh*

Perhaps	Quizá *keethah*
I don't know	No lo sé *noh loh seh*

2.4 Thank you

Thank you	Gracias *grahthyahs*
You're welcome	De nada *deh nahdah*
Thank you very much	Muchísimas gracias *moocheeseemahs grahthyahs*
Very kind of you	Muy amable (de su parte) *mwee ahmahbleh (deh soo pahrteh)*
I enjoyed it very much	Ha sido un verdadero placer *ah seedoh oon behrdahdehroh plahthehr*
Thank you for your trouble	Gracias por la molestia *grahthyahs pohr lah mohlehstyah*
You shouldn't have	No se hubiera molestado *noh seh oobyehrah mohlehstahdoh*
That's all right	No se preocupe *noh seh prehohkoopeh*

2.5 Sorry

Excuse me	Perdone *pehrdohneh*
Sorry!	¡Perdone! *pehrdohneh!*
I'm sorry, I didn't know...	Perdone, no sabía que... *pehrdohneh, noh sahbeeah keh...*
I do apologise	Perdone *pehrdohneh*

I'm sorry	**Lo siento** *loh syehntoh*
I didn't do it on purpose, it was an accident	**No ha sido a propósito; ha sido sin querer** *noh ah seedoh ah prohpohseetoh; ah seedoh seen kehrehr*
That's all right	**No importa** *noh eempohrtah*
Never mind	**Déjelo** *dehhehloh*
It could've happened to anyone	**Le puede pasar a cualquiera** *leh pwehdeh pahsahr ah kwahlkyehrah*

2.6 What do you think?

Which do you prefer?	**¿Qué prefiere?** *keh prehfyehreh?*
What do you think?	**¿Qué te parece?** *keh teh pahrehtheh?*
Don't you like dancing?	**¿No te gusta bailar?** *noh teh goostah bahylahr?*
I don't mind	**Me da igual** *meh dah eegwahl*
Well done!	**¡Muy bien!** *mwee byehn!*
Not bad!	**¡No está mal!** *noh ehstah mahl!*
Great!	**¡Excelente!** *ehxthehlehnteh!*
Wonderful!	**¡Qué delicia!** *keh dehleethyah!*
It's really nice here!	**¡Qué bien se está aquí!** *keh byehn seh ehstah ahkee!*
How nice!	**¡Qué mono/bonito!** *keh mohnoh/bohneetoh!*

How nice for you!	¡Cuánto me alegro por usted! *kwahntoh meh ahlehgroh pohr oostehdh!*
I'm (not) very happy with...	(No) estoy muy contento con... *(noh) ehstoy mwee kohntehntoh kohn...*
I'm glad...	Me alegro de que... *meh ahlehgroh deh keh...*
I'm having a great time	Me lo estoy pasando muy bien *meh loh ehstoy pahsahndoh mwee byehn*
I'm looking forward to it	Me hace ilusión *meh ahtheh eeloosyohn*
I hope it'll work out	Espero que salga bien *ehspehroh keh sahlgah byehn*
That's ridiculous!	¡Qué ridículo! *keh reedeekooloh!*
That's terrible!	¡Qué horrible! *keh ohrreebleh!*
What a pity!	¡Qué lástima! *keh lahsteemah!*
That's filthy!	¡Qué asco! *keh ahskoh!*
What a load of rubbish!	¡Qué tontería! *keh tohntehreeah!*
I don't like...	No me gusta... *noh meh goostah...*
I'm bored to death	Me aburro como una ostra *meh ahboorroh kohmoh oonah ohstrah*
I've had enough	Estoy harto(a) *ehstoy ahrtoh(ah)*
This is no good	No puede ser *noh pwehdeh sehr*
I was expecting something completely different	Yo me había esperado otra cosa *yoh meh ahbeeah ehspehrahdoh ohtrah kohsah*

3

Conversation

3.1 I beg your pardon?

I don't speak any/ I speak a little...	No hablo/hablo un poco de... *noh ahbloh/ahbloh oon pohkoh deh...*
I'm English	Soy inglés/inglesa *soy eenglehs/eenglehsah*
I'm Scottish	Soy escocés/escocesa *soy ehskohthehs/ehskothehsah*
I'm Irish	Soy irlandés/irlandesa *soy eerlahndehs/eerlahndehsah*
I'm Welsh	soy galés/galesa *soy gahlehs/gahlehsah*
Do you speak English/French/ German?	¿Habla inglés/francés/alemán? *ahblah eenglehs/frahnthehs/ahlehmahn?*
Is there anyone who speaks...?	¿Hay alguien que hable...? *ay ahlgyehn ahkee keh ahbleh...?*
I beg your pardon?	¿Cómo dice? *kohmoh deetheh?*
I (don't) understand	(No) comprendo *(noh) kohmprehndoh*
Do you understand me?	¿Me entiende? *meh ehntyehndeh?*
Could you repeat that, please?	¿Le importa repetirlo? *leh eempohrtah rehpehteerloh?*
Could you speak more slowly, please?	¿Podría hablar más despacio? *pohdreeah ahblahr mahs dehspahthyo?*
What does that (word) mean?	¿Qué significa esto/esta palabra? *keh seegneefeekah ehstoh/ehstah pahlahbrah?*
Is that similar to/the same as...?	¿Es (más o menos) lo mismo que...? *ehs mahs oh mehnohs loh meesmoh keh...?*
Could you write that down for me, please?	¿Podría escribírmelo? *pohdreeah eskreebeermehloh?*

Could you spell that for me, please?	**¿Podría deletreármelo?** *pohdreeah dehlehtrehahrmehloh?*

(See 1.8 Telephone alphabet)

Could you point that out in this phrase book, please?	**¿Me lo podría señalar en esta guía?** *meh loh pohdreeah sehnyahlahr ehn ehstah gheeah?*
One moment, please, I have to look it up	**Espere que lo busco en la guía** *ehspehreh keh loh booskoh ehn lah gheeah*
I can't find the word/the sentence	**No puedo encontrar la palabra/la frase** *noh pwehdoh ehnkohntrahr lah pahlahbrah/lah frahseh*
How do you say that in...?	**¿Cómo se dice eso en...?** *kohmoh seh deetheh ehstoh ehn...?*
How do you pronounce that?	**¿Cómo se pronuncia?** *kohmoh seh prohnoonthyah?*

3.2 Introductions

May I introduce myself?	**Permítame presentarme** *pehrmeetahmeh prehsehntahrmeh*
My name's...	**Me llamo...** *meh lyahmoh...*
I'm...	**Soy...** *soy...*
What's your name?	**¿Cómo se llama?** *kohmoh seh lyahmah?*
May I introduce...?	**Permítame presentarle a...** *pehrmeetahmeh prehsehntahrleh ah...*
This is my wife/daughter/mother/girlfriend	**Esta es mi mujer/mi hija/mi madre/mi amiga** *ehstah ehs mee moohehr/mee eehah /mee mahdreh/mee ahmeegah*

– my husband/son/ father/boyfriend.	**Este es mi marido/mi hijo/mi padre/mi amigo** *ehsteh ehs mee mahreedoh/mee eehoh/mee pahdreh/mee ahmeegoh*
How do you do	**Hola, mucho gusto** *ohlah, moochoh goostoh*
Pleased to meet you	**Encantado(a) (de conocerle)** *ehnkahntahdoh(ah) (deh kohnohthehrleh)*
Where are you from?	**¿De dónde es usted?** *deh dohndeh ehs oostehdh?*
I'm from England/Scotland/ Ireland/Wales	**Soy inglés/esa escocés/esa irlandés/esa galés/esa** *soy eenglehs/ehsah ehskohthehs/ehsah eerlahndehs/ehsah gahlehs/ ehsah*
What city do you live in?	**¿En qué ciudad vive?** *ehn keh thyoodahdh beebeh?*
In..., It's near...	**En...Eso está cerca de...** *ehn...ehsoh ehstah thehrkah deh...*
Have you been here long?	**¿Hace mucho que está aquí?** *ahtheh moochoh keh ehstah ahkee?*
A few days	**Unos días** *oonohs deeahs*
How long are you staying here?	**¿Cuánto tiempo piensa quedarse?** *kwahntoh tyehmpoh pyehnsah kehdahrseh?*
We're (probably) leaving tomorrow/ in two weeks	**Nos iremos (probablemente) mañana/dentro de dos semanas** *nohs eerehmohs (prohbahblehmehnteh) mahnyahnah/dehntroh deh dohs sehmahnahs*
Where are you staying?	**¿Dónde se aloja?** *dohndeh seh ahlohhah?*
In a hotel/an apartment	**En un hotel/apartamento** *ehn oon ohtehl/ahpahrtahmehntoh*
On a camp site	**En un camping** *ehn oon kahmpeen*

With friends/relatives	En casa de amigos/parientes *ehn kahsah deh ahmeegohs/pahryehntehs*
Are you here on your own/with your family?	¿Ha venido solo(a)/con su familia? *ah behneedoh sohloh(ah)/kohn soo fahmeelyah?*
I'm on my own	He venido solo(a) *eh behneedoh sohloh(ah)*
I'm with my partner/wife/husband	con mi pareja/mujer/marido *kohn mee pahrehhah/moohehr/mahreedoh*
– with my family	con mi familia *kohn mee fahmeelyah*
– with relatives	con unos parientes *kohn oonohs pahryehntehs*
– with a friend/friends	con un amigo/una amiga/unos amigos *kohn oon ahmeegoh/oonah ahmeegah/oonohs ahmeegohs*
Are you married?	¿Está casado/casada? *ehstah kahsahdoh/kahsahdah?*
Do you have a steady boyfriend/girlfriend?	¿Tienes novio/novia? *tyehnehs nohbyoh/nohbyah?*
That's none of your business.	No es asunto suyo *noh ehs ahsoontoh sooyoh*
I'm married	Soy casado *soy kahsahdoh*
– single	Soy soltero *soy sohltehroh*
– separated	Estoy separado *ehstoy sehpahrahdoh*
– divorced	Estoy divorciado *ehstoy deebohrthyahdoh*
– a widow/widower	Soy viuda/viudo *soy byoodah/byoodoh*
I live alone/with someone	Vivo solo(a)/con otra persona *beeboh sohloh(ah)/kohn ohtrah pehrsohnah*
Do you have any children/grandchildren	¿Tiene hijos/nietos? *tyehneh eehohs/nyehtohs?*

How old are you?	¿Cuántos años tiene? *kwahntohs ahnyohs tyehneh?*
How old is she/he?	¿Cuántos años tiene? *kwahntohs ahnyohs tyehneh?*
I'm...	Tengo...años *tehngoh...ahnyohs*
She's/he's...	Tiene...años *tyehneh...ahnyohs*
What do you do for a living?	¿En qué trabaja? *ehn keh trahbahhah?*
I work in an office	Trabajo en una oficina *trahbahhoh ehn oonah ohfeetheenah*
I'm a student/ I'm at school	Estudio *ehstoodyoh*
I'm unemployed	Estoy en paro *ehstoy ehn pahroh*
I'm retired	Soy jubilado *soy hoobeelahdoh*
I'm on a disability pension	Tengo una pensión de invalidez *tehngoh oonah pehnsyohn deh eenbahleedeth*
I'm a housewife	Soy ama de casa *soy ahmah deh kahsah*
Do you like your job?	¿Le gusta su trabajo? *leh goostah soo trahbahhoh?*
Most of the time	A veces sí, a veces no *ah behthehs see, ah behthehs noh*
I usually do, but I prefer holidays	Por lo general sí, pero prefiero las vacaciones *pohr loh hehnehrahl see, pehroh prehfyehroh lahs bahkahthyohnehs*

3.3 Starting/ending a conversation

Could I ask you something?	¿Podría preguntarle una cosa? *pohdreeah prehgoontahrleh oonah kohsah?*
Excuse me	Perdone *pehrdohneh*
Excuse me, could you help me?	¿Podría ayudarme? *pohdreeah ahyoodahrmeh?*
Yes, what's the problem?	Sí, ¿qué pasa? *see, keh pahsah?*
What can I do for you?	¿En qué puedo servirle? *ehn keh pwehdoh sehrbeerleh?*
Sorry, I don't have time now	Lo siento, ahora no tengo tiempo *loh syehntoh, ahohrah noh tehngoh tyehmpoh*
Do you have a light?	¿Tiene fuego? *tyehneh fwehgoh?*
May I join you?	¿Le importa que me siente? *leh eempohrtah keh meh syehnteh?*
Could you take a picture of me/us? Press this button.	¿Podría sacarme/sacarnos una foto? Hay que apretar este botón *pohdreeah sahkahrmeh/sahkahrnohs oonah fohtoh? ay keh ahprehtahr ehsteh bohtohn*
Leave me alone	Déjeme en paz *dehhehmeh ehn pahth*
Get lost	Váyase al diablo *bahyahseh ahl deeahbloh*
Go away or I'll scream	Como no se vaya, grito *kohmoh noh seh bahyah, greetoh*

3.4 Congratulations and condolences

Happy birthday/many happy returns	Feliz cumpleaños/felicidades *fehleeth koomplehahnyohs/fehleetheedahdehs*
Please accept my condolences.	Le acompaño en el sentimiento *leh ahkohmpahnyoh ehn ehl sehnteemyehntoh*
I'm very sorry for you	¡Cuánto lo siento por usted! *kwahntoh loh syehntoh pohr oostehdh!*

3.5 A chat about the weather

See also 1.5 The weather

It's so hot/cold today!	¡Qué calor/frío hace hoy! *keh kahlohr/freeoh ahtheh oy!*
Nice weather, isn't it?	¡Qué buen tiempo hace! ¿Verdad? *keh bwehn tyehmpoh ahtheh! behrdah?*
What a wind/storm!	¡Vaya viento/tormenta! *bahyah byehntoh/tohrmentah!*
All that rain/snow!	¡Cómo llueve/nieva! *kohmoh lywehbeh/nyehbah!*
All that fog!	¡Cuánta niebla! *kwahntah nyehblah!*
Has the weather been like this for long here?	¿Hace mucho que hace este tiempo? *ahtheh moochoh keh ahtheh ehsteh tyehmpoh?*
Is it always this hot/cold here?	¿Aquí siempre hace tanto calor/frío? *ahkee syehmpreh ahtheh tahntoh kahlohr/freeoh?*
Is it always this dry/wet here?	¿Aquí siempre hace un tiempo tan seco/lluvioso? *ahkee syehmpreh ahtheh oon tyehmpoh tahn sehkoh/lyoobyohsoh?*

3.6 Hobbies

Do you have any hobbies?	**¿Tiene algún hobby?** *tyehneh algoon hohbee?*
I like painting/reading/photography/DIY	**Me gusta pintar/leer/la fotografía/el bricolaje** *meh goostah peentahr/lehehr/lah fohtohgrahfeeah/ehl breekohlahheh*
I like music	**Me gusta la música** *meh goostah lah mooseekah*
I like playing the guitar/piano	**Me gusta tocar la guitarra/el piano** *meh goostah tohkahr lah gueetahrrah/ehl pyahnoh*
I like going to the movies	**Me gusta ir al cine** *meh goostah eer ahl theeneh*
I like travelling/sport/fishing/walking	**Me gusta viajar/hacer deporte/pescar/salir a caminar** *meh goostah byahhahr/ahthehr dehpohrteh/pehskahr/sahleer ah kahmeenahr*

3.7 Being the host(ess)

See also 4 Eating out

Can I offer you a drink?	**¿Le gustaría algo de beber?** *leh goostahreeah ahlgoh deh behbehr?*
What would you like to drink?	**¿Qué quieres beber?** *keh kyehrehs behbehr?*
Something non-alcoholic, please.	**Algo sin alcohol** *ahlgoh seen ahlkohl*

Would you like a cigarette/cigar/to roll your own?	¿Quiere un cigarrillo/un puro/liar un cigarrillo? *kyehreh oon theegahrreelyoh/oon pooroh/leeahr oon theegahrreelyoh?*
I don't smoke	No fumo *noh foomoh*

3.8 Invitations

Are you doing anything tonight?	¿Tiene algo que hacer esta noche? *tyehneh ahlgoh keh ahthehr ehstah nohcheh?*
Do you have any plans for today/this afternoon/tonight?	¿Ya tiene planes para hoy/esta tarde/esta noche? *yah tyehneh plahnehs pahrah oy/ehstah tahrdeh/ehstah nohcheh?*
Would you like to go out with me?	¿Le(te) apetece salir conmigo? *leh(teh) ahpehtehtheh sahleer kohnmeegoh?*
Would you like to go dancing with me?	¿Le(te) apetece ir a bailar conmigo? *leh(teh) ahpehtehtheh eer ah baylahr kohnmeegoh?*
Would you like to have lunch/dinner with me?	¿Le(te) apetece comer/cenar conmigo? *leh(teh) ahpehtehtheh kohmehr/thenahr kohnmeegoh?*
Would you like to come to the beach with me?	¿Le(te) apetece ir a la playa conmigo? *leh(teh) ahpehtehtheh eer ah lah plahyah kohnmeegoh?*
Would you like to comeinto town with us?	¿Le apetece ir a la ciudad con nosotros? *leh ahpehtehtheh eer ah lah thyoodahdh kohn nohsohtrohs?*
Would you like to come and see some friends with us?	¿Le apetece ir a casa de unos amigos con nosotros? *leh ahpehtehtheh eer ah kahsah deh oonohs ahmeegohs kohn nohsohtrohs?*

Shall we dance?	**¿Bailamos?** *baylahmohs?*
– sit at the bar?	**¿Vienes a sentarte conmigo en la barra?** *byehnehs ah sehntahrteh kohnmeegoh ehn lah bahrrah?*
– get something to drink?	**¿Vamos a beber algo?** *bahmohs ah behbehr ahlgoh?*
– go for a walk/drive?	**¿Vamos a dar una vuelta?** *bahmohs ah dahr oonah bwehltah?*
Yes, all right	**Sí, vamos** *see, bahmohs*
Good idea	**Buena idea** *bwehnah eedehah*
No (thank you)	**No (gracias)** *noh (grahthyahs)*
Maybe later	**Quizá más tarde** *keethah mahs tahrdeh*
I don't feel like it	**No me apetece** *noh meh ahpehtehtheh*
I don't have time	**No tengo tiempo** *noh tehngoh tyehmpoh*
I already have a date	**Ya tengo otro compromiso** *yah tehngoh ohtroh kohmprohmeesoh*
I'm not very good at dancing/volleyball/ swimming	**No sé bailar/jugar al vóleibol/nadar** *noh seh baylahr/hoogahr ahl vohleheebohl/nahdahr*

3.9 Paying a compliment

You look wonderful!	**¡Qué guapo/guapa está(estás)!** *keh wahpoh/wahpah ehstah(ehstahs)!*
I like your car!	**¡Qué bonito coche!** *keh bohneetoh kohcheh!*
I like your ski outfit!	**¡Qué bonito traje de esquiar!** *keh bohneetoh trahheh deh ehskeeahr!*

You're a nice boy/girl	Eres muy bueno/buena *ehrehs mwee bwehnoh/bwehnah*
What a sweet child!	¡Qué niño tan majo/niña tan maja! *keh neenyoh tahn mahhoh/neenyah tahn mahhah!*
You're a wonderful dancer!	Bailas muy bien *bahylahs mwee byehn*
You're a wonderful cook!	Cocinas muy bien *kohtheenahs mwee byehn*
You're a terrific soccer player!	Juegas muy bien al fútbol *hwehgahs mwee byehn ahl footbohl*

3.10 Chatting someone up

I like being with you	Me gusta estar contigo *meh goostah ehstahr kohnteegoh*
I've missed you so much	Te he echado mucho de menos *teh eh ehchahdoh moochoh deh mehnohs*
I dreamt about you	He soñado contigo *eh sohnyahdoh kohnteegoh*
I think about you all day	Pienso todo el día en ti *pyehnsoh tohdoh ehl deeah ehn tee*
You have such a sweet smile	Tienes una sonrisa muy bonita *tyehnehs oonah sohnreesah mwee bohneetah*
You have such beautiful eyes	Tienes unos ojos muy bonitos *tyehnehs oonohs ohhohs mwee bohneetohs*
I'm in love with you	Estoy enamorado/enamorada de ti *ehstoy ehnahmohrahdoh/ehnahmohrahdah deh tee*
I'm in love with you too	Yo también de ti *yoh tahmbyehn deh tee*
I love you	Te quiero *teh kyehroh*

I love you too	Yo también a ti *yoh tahmbyehn ah tee*
I don't feel as strongly about you	Yo no siento lo mismo por ti *yoh noh syehntoh loh meesmoh pohr tee*
I already have a boyfriend/girlfriend	Ya tengo pareja *yah tehngoh pahrehhah*
I'm not ready for that	Yo no estoy preparado(a) *yoh noh ehstoy prehpahrahdoh/ah*
This is going too fast for me	Vamos demasiado rápido *bahmohs dehmahsyahdoh rahpeedoh*
Take your hands off me	No me toque(s) *noh meh tohkeh(s)*
Okay, no problem	Vale, no importa *bahleh, noh eempohrtah*
Will you stay with me tonight?	¿Te quedas a dormir? *teh kehdahs ah dohrmeer?*
I'd like to go to bed with you	Me gustaría acostarme contigo *meh goostahreeah ahkohstahrmeh kohnteegoh*
Only if we use a condom	Sólo si usamos condón *sohloh see oosahmohs kohndohn*
We have to be careful about AIDS	Hay que tener cuidado por lo del Sida *ay keh tehnehr kweedahdoh pohr loh dehl seedah*
That's what they all say	Eso es lo que dicen todos *ehsoh ehs loh keh deethehn tohdohs*
We shouldn't take any risks	Más vale no arriesgarse *mahs bahleh noh ahrryehsgahrseh*
Do you have a condom?	¿Llevas condones? *lyehbahs kohndohnehs?*
No? In that case we won't do it	¿No? Pues entonces no *noh? pwehs ehntohnthehs noh*

3.11 Arrangements

When will I see you again?	**¿Cuándo te veo?** *kwahndoh teh behoh?*
Are you free over the weekend?	**¿Tiene tiempo este fin de semana?** *tyehneh tyehmpoh ehsteh feen deh sehmahnah?*
What shall we arrange?	**¿Cómo quedamos?** *kohmoh kehdahmohs?*
Where shall we meet?	**¿Dónde nos encontramos?** *dohndeh nohs ehnkohntrahmohs?*
Will you pick me/us up?	**¿Me/nos pasa a buscar?** *meh/nohs pahsah ah booskahr?*
Shall I pick you up?	**¿Lo/la paso a buscar?** *loh/lah pahsoh ah booskahr?*
I have to be home by...	**Tengo que estar en casa a las...** *tehngoh keh ehstahr ehn kahsah ah lahs...*
I don't want to see you anymore	**No quiero volver a verlo/verla** *noh kyehroh bohlbehr ah behrloh/behrlah*

3.12 Saying goodbye

Can I take you home?	**¿Lo/la acompaño a su casa?** *loh/lah ahkohmpahnyoh ah soo kahsah?*
Can I write/call you?	**¿Puedo escribirle/llamarlo/llamarla por teléfono?** *pwehdoh ehskreebeerleh /lyahmahrloh/ lyahmahrlah pohr tehlehfohnoh?*
Will you write/call me?	**¿Me escribirá/llamará por teléfono?** *meh ehskreebeerah/lyahmahrah pohr tehlehfohnoh?*
Can I have your address/phone number?	**¿Me da su dirección/número de teléfono?** *meh dah soo deerehkthyohn/noomehroh deh tehlehfohnoh?*

Thanks for everything	Gracias por todo *grahthyahs pohr tohdoh*
It was very nice	Lo hemos pasado muy bien *loh ehmohs pahsahdoh mwee byehn*
Say hello to...	Recuerdos a... *rehkwehrdohs ah...*
All the best	Te deseo lo mejor *teh dehsehoh loh mehhohr*
Good luck	Que te vaya bien *keh teh bahyah byehn*
When will you be back?	¿Cuándo vuelves? *kwahndoh bwehlbehs?*
I'll be waiting for you	Te esperaré *teh ehspehrahreh.*
I'd like to see you again	Me gustaría volver a verte *meh goostahreeah bohlbehr ah behrteh*
I hope we meet again soon	Espero que nos volvamos a ver pronto *ehspehroh keh nohs bohlbahmohs ah behr prohntoh*
This is our address. If you're ever in the UK	Esta es nuestra dirección. Si alguna vez pasa por el Reino Unido... *ehstah ehs nwehstrah deerehkthyohn. see ahlgoonah behth pahsah pohr ehl reheenoh ooneedoh...*
You'd be more than welcome	Está cordialmente invitado *ehstah kohrdyahlmehnteh eenbeetahdoh*

4 Eating out

● **In Spain** people usually have three meals:
1 *El desayuno* (breakfast) approximately between 7 and 10am. Breakfast is light and consists of *café con leche* (white coffee), a croissant or *suizo* (light sugary bun) or *tostadas* (toast).
2 *El almuerzo* (lunch) approx. between 2 and 4pm, though hotels usually serve at standard times. Lunch always includes a hot dish and is the most important meal of the day. Office workers and schoolchildren still lunch at home. It usually consists of four courses:
- starter (which can be a plate of greens)
- main course
- dessert
- fruit

3 *La cena* (dinner) between 9 and 11pm, 8pm in most hotels. Dinner is usually a light, hot meal, taken with the family.
At around 6 or 7pm, a snack (*la merienda*) is often served, consisting frequently of sandwiches with *chorizo* or *jamón serrano* and *pastas* (biscuits) or small cakes.
Pinchos and *tapas* are often taken at bars with an apéritif, either in the late morning or the evening.

4.1 On arrival

I'd like to book a table for seven o'clock, please	**¿Podría reservar una mesa para las siete?** *pohdreeah rehsehrbahr oonah mehsah pahrah lahs syehteh?*
I'd like a table for two, please	**Quisiera una mesa para dos personas** *keesyehrah oonah mehsah pahrah dohs pehrsohnahs*
We've/we haven't booked	**(No) hemos reservado** *(noh) ehmohs rehsehrbahdoh*
Is the restaurant open yet?	**¿Ya está abierto el restaurante?** *yah ehstah ahbyehrtoh ehl rehstahoorahnteh?*

¿Ha reservado mesa?	Do you have a reservation?
¿A nombre de quién?	What name, please?
Por aquí, por favor.	This way, please
Esta mesa está reservada	This table is reserved
En quince minutos quedará libre una mesa	We'll have a table free in fifteen minutes.
¿Le importaría esperar (en la barra)?	Would you like to wait (at the bar)?

What time does the restaurant open/close? ¿A qué hora abre/cierra el restaurante?
ah keh ohrah ahbreh/thyehrrah ehl rehstahoorahnteh?

Can we wait for a table? ¿Podemos esperar hasta que se desocupe una mesa?
pohdehmohs ehspehrahr ahstah keh seh dehsohkoopeh oonah mehsah?

Do we have to wait long? ¿Tenemos que esperar mucho?
tehnehmohs keh ehspehrahr moochoh?

Is this seat taken? ¿Está ocupada esta silla?
ehstah ohkoopahdah ehstah seelyah?

Could we sit here/there? ¿Podemos sentarnos aquí/allí?
pohdemohs sehntahrnohs ahkee/ahlyee?

Can we sit by the window? ¿Podemos sentarnos junto a la ventana?
pohdehmohs sehntahrnohs hoontoh ah lah behntahnah?

Can we eat outside? ¿Podemos comer afuera?
pohdehmohs kohmehr ahfwehrah?

Do you have another chair for us? ¿Podría traernos otra silla?
pohdreeah trahehrnohs ohtrah seelyah?

Do you have a highchair? ¿Podría traernos una silla para niños?
pohdreeah trahehrnohs oonah seelyah pahrah neenyohs?

Is there a socket for this bottle-warmer? ___ ¿Hay un enchufe para este calentador de biberones?
ay oon ehnchoofeh pahrah ehsteh kahlehntahdohr deh beebehrohnehs?

Could you warm up this bottle/jar for me? ___ ¿Podría calentarme este biberón/este bote?
pohdreeah kahlehntahrmeh ehsteh beebehrohn/ehsteh bohteh?

Not too hot, please ___ Que no esté muy caliente, por favor
keh noh ehsteh mwee kahlyehnteh pohr fahbohr

Is there somewhere I can change the baby's nappy? ___ ¿Hay algún lugar para cambiar al bebé?
ay ahlgoon loogahr pahrah kahmbyahr ahl behbeh?

Where are the toilets? ___ ¿Dónde están los servicios?
dohnde ehstahn lohs sehrbeethyohs?

4.2 Ordering

Waiter! ___ ¡Camarero!
kahmahrehroh!

Madam!/Sir! ___ ¡Oiga, (por favor)!
oygah (pohr fahbohr)!

We'd like something to eat/a drink ___ Quisiéramos comer/beber algo
keesyehrahmohs kohmehr/behber ahlgoh

Could I have a quick meal? ___ ¿Podría comer algo rápido?
pohdreeah kohmehr ahlgoh rahpeedoh?

We don't have much time ___ Tenemos poco tiempo
tehnehmohs pohkoh tyehmpoh

We'd like to have a drink first ___ Antes quisiéramos beber algo
ahntehs keesyehrahmohs behbehr ahlgoh

Could we see the menu/wine list, please? ___ ¿Nos podría traer la carta/la carta de vinos?
nohs pohdreeah trahehr lah kahrtah/lah kahrtah deh beenohs?

Do you have a menu in English?	¿Tienen menú en inglés? *tyehnehn mehnoo ehn eenglehs?*
Do you have a dish of the day?	¿Tienen menú del día/menú turístico? *tyehnehn mehnoo dehl deeah/mehnoo tooreesteekoh?*
We haven't made a choice yet	Todavía no hemos elegido *tohdahbeeah noh ehmohs ehlehheedoh*
What do you recommend?	¿Qué nos recomienda? *keh nohs rehkohmyehndah?*
What are the specialities of the region/the house?	¿Cuáles son las especialidades de la región/de la casa? *kwahlehs sohn lahs ehspehthyahleedahdehs deh lah rehhyohn/deh lah kahsah?*
I like strawberries/ olives	Me gustan las fresas/las aceitunas *meh goostahn lahs frehsahs/lahs ahtheheetoonahs*
I don't like meat/fish/...	No me gusta el pescado/la carne/... *noh meh goostah ehl pehskahdoh/lah kahrneh/...*
What's this?	¿Qué es esto? *keh ehs ehstoh?*

¿Van a tomar un aperitivo?	Would you like a drink first?
¿Ya han elegido?	Have you decided?
¿Qué van a tomar?	What would you like to eat?
Que aproveche	Enjoy your meal.
¿Quiere su bistec rojo, mediano o muy hecho?	Would you like your steak rare, medium or well done?
¿Van a tomar postre/café?	Would you like a dessert/coffee?

Does it have...in it?	¿Lleva...? *lyehbah...?*
What does it taste like?	¿A qué sabe? *ah keh sahbeh?*
Is this a hot or a cold dish?	¿Es un plato caliente o frío? *ehs oon plahtoh kahlyehnteh oh freeoh?*
Is this sweet?	¿Es un plato dulce? *ehs oon plahtoh doolthe?*
Is this spicy?	¿Es un plato picante? *ehs oon plahtoh peekahnteh?*
Do you have anything else, please?	¿Tendría otra cosa? *tehndreeah ohtrah kohsah?*
I'm on a salt-free diet	No puedo comer sal *noh pwehdoh kohmehr sahl*
I can't eat pork	No puedo comer carne de cerdo *noh pwehdoh kohmehr kahrneh deh thehrdoh*
– sugar	No puedo comer azúcar *noh pwehdo kohmehr ahthookahr*
– fatty foods	No puedo comer grasa *noh pwehdoh kohmehr grahsah*
– (hot) spices	No puedo comer cosas picantes *noh pwehdoh kohmehr kohsahs peekahntehs*
I'll/we'll have what those people are having	Lo mismo que esos señores, por favor *loh meesmoh keh ehsohs sehnyohrehs pohr fahbohr*
I'd like...	Para mí... *pahrah mee...*
We're not having a starter	No vamos a comer primer plato *noh bahmohs ah kohmehr preemehr plahtoh*
The child will share what we're having	El niño/la niña comerá de nuestro menú *ehl neenyoh/lah neenyah kohmehrah deh nwehstroh mehnoo*

Could I have some more bread, please?	Más pan, por favor *mahs pahn pohr fahbohr*
– a bottle of water/ wine	Otra botella de agua/de vino, por favor *ohtrah bohtehlyah deh ahgwah/deh beenoh, pohr fahbohr*
– another helping of...	Otra ración de..., por favor *ohtrah rahthyohn deh..., pohr fahbohr*
– some salt and pepper	¿Podría traerme sal y pimienta? *pohdreeah trahehrmeh sahl ee peemyehntah?*
– a napkin	¿Podría traerme una servilleta? *pohdreeah trahehrmeh oonah sehrbeelyehtah?*
– a spoon	¿Podría traerme una cuchara? *pohdreeah trahehrmeh oonah koochahrah?*
– an ashtray	¿Podría traerme un cenicero? *pohdreeah trahehrmeh oon thehneethehroh?*
– some matches	¿Podría traerme unas cerillas? *pohdreeah trahehrmeh oonahs thehreelyahs?*
– some toothpicks	¿Podría traerme unos palillos? *pohdreeah trahehrmeh oonohs pahleelyohs?*
– a glass of water	¿Podría traerme un vaso de agua? *pohdreeah trahehrmeh oon bahsoh deh ahgwah?*
– a straw (for the child)	¿Podría traerme una pajita (para el niño/ la niña)? *pohdreeah trahehrmeh oonah pahheetah (pahrah ehl neenyoh/lah neenyah)?*
Enjoy your meal!	¡Que aproveche! *keh ahprohbehcheh!*
You too!	Igualmente *eegwahlmehnteh*
Cheers!	¡Salud! *sahloodh!*

The next round's on me	La próxima ronda la pago yo *lah prohxeemah rohndah lah pahgoh yoh*
Could we have a doggy bag, please?	¿Podemos llevarnos las sobras? *pohdehmohs lyehbarnohs lahs sohbrahs?*

4.3 The bill

See also 8.2 Settling the bill

How much is this dish?	¿Cuánto vale este plato? *kwahntoh bahleh ehsteh plahtoh?*
Could I have the bill, please?	La cuenta, por favor *lah kwehntah, pohr fahbohr*
All together	Todo junto *tohdoh hoontoh*
Everyone pays separately	Cada uno paga lo suyo *kahdah oonoh pahgah loh sooyoh*
Could we have the menu again, please?	¿Podría traernos otra vez la carta? *pohdreeah trahehrnohs ohtrah behth lah kahrtah?*
The...is not on the bill	Ha olvidado apuntar el/la... *ah olbeedahdoh ahpoontahr ehl/lah...*

4.4 Complaints

It's taking a very long time	Están tardando mucho *ehstahn tahrdahndoh moochoh*
We've been here an hour already	Ya llevamos una hora aquí *yah lyebahmohs oonah ohrah ahkee*
This must be a mistake	Esto tiene que ser una equivocación *ehstoh tyehneh keh sehr oonah ehkeebohkahthyohn*

This is not what I ordered	**Esto no es lo que he pedido** *ehstoh noh ehs loh keh eh pehdeedoh*
I ordered...	**He pedido...** *eh pehdeedoh*
There's a dish missing	**Falta un plato** *fahltah oon plahtoh*
This is broken/ not clean	**Esto está roto/no está limpio** *ehstoh ehstah rohtoh/noh ehstah leempyoh*
The food's cold	**La comida está fría** *lah kohmeedah ehstah freeah*
– not fresh	**La comida no es fresca** *lah kohmeedah noh ehs frehskah*
– too salty/sweet/spicy	**La comida está muy salada/dulce/picante** *lah kohmeedah ehstah mwee sahlahdah/doolteh/peekahnteh*
The meat's not done	**La carne está cruda** *lah kahrneh ehstah kroodah*
– overdone	**La carne está muy hecha** *lah kahrneh ehstah mwee ehchah*
– tough	**La carne está dura** *lah kahrneh ehstah doorah*
– off	**La carne está podrida** *lah kahrneh ehstah pohdreedah*
Could I have something else instead of this?	**¿Me podría traer otra cosa en lugar de esto?** *meh pohdreeah trahehr ohtrah kohsah ehn loogahr deh ehstoh?*
The bill/this amount is not right	**La cuenta/este precio está mal** *lah kwehntah/ehsteh prehthyoh ehstah mahl*
We didn't have this	**Esto no lo hemos comido/bebido** *ehstoh noh loh ehmohs kohmeedoh/behbeedoh*
There's no paper in the toilet	**No hay papel en el servicio** *noh ay pahpehl ehn ehl sehrbeethyoh*
Do you have a complaints book?	**¿Tienen libro de quejas?** *tyehnen leebroh deh kehhas?*

Will you call the manager, please?	**Haga el favor de llamar al jefe** *ahgah ehl fahbohr deh lyamahr ahl hehfeh*

4.5 Paying a compliment

That was a wonderful meal	**Hemos comido muy bien** *ehmohs kohmeedoh mwee byehn*
The food was excellent	**La comida ha estado exquisita** *lah kohmeedah ah ehstahdoh ehxkeeseetah*
The...in particular was delicious	**Sobre todo nos ha gustado el/la...** *sohbreh tohdoh nohs ah goostahdoh ehl/lah...*

4.6 The menu

aperitivo apéritif
aves poultry
azúcar
sugar
bebidas alcohólicas
alcoholic beverages
bebidas calientes
hot beverages
carta de vinos
wine list
cócteles cocktails
cubierto
cover charge
entremeses variados
hors d'oeuvres
mariscos seafood
pastelería
pastry
pescados
fish
platos calientes
hot dishes
platos combinados
combined dishes
plato del día
dish of the day
platos fríos
cold dishes
platos principales
main courses
platos típicos
regional specialities
postres
sweets/dessert
primeros platos
starters
raciones
portions
servicio incluido
service included
sopas
soups
tapas
tapas
venado
game
verduras
vegetables

4.7 Alphabetical list of drinks and dishes

aceituna
olive
aguacate
avocado
ajo
garlic
albóndigas
meat balls
alcachofa
artichoke
almejas
clams
almendras
almonds
ancas de rana
frog's legs
anchoa/boquerón
anchovy
anguila
eel
anís
aniseed
apio
celery
arenque
herring
arroz
rice
asado
roast, roasted
atún/bonito
tuna
avellana
hazelnut
bacalao
cod
batido de...
milk shake
berenjena
aubergine
biftec
steak
bizcocho (borracho)
sponge cake(with sherry or similar)
bocadillo
sandwich
buey/vaca
beef
cabrito
kid
café (solo/con leche)
coffee (black/white)
calamares (en su tinta)
squid (cooked in their ink)
caldo
broth
callos
tripe
cangrejo
crab
caracoles
snails
carne
meat
carpa
carp
castaña
chestnut
cebolla
onion
cerdo
pork
cerezas
cherries
cerveza
beer
chorizo
chorizo (paprika flavoured salami sausage)
chucrut
sauerkraut
chuleta/costilla
chop
churros
fritters
ciervo
venison
cigalas
Dublin Bay prawns
ciruela
plum

cochinillo asado
roast suckling pig
cocido
boiled
codorniz
quail
col/berza
cabbage
coles de Bruselas
Brussels sprouts
coliflor
cauliflower
coñac
brandy
conejo
rabbit
copa helada/helado
ice cream
cordero
lamb
crema/nata
cream
criadillas/mollejas
sweetbreads
crudo
raw
cuba libre
rum coke
dátil
date
dulce
sweet

emperador
swordfish
en escabeche
pickled
endibia
chicory/endive
ensalada (mixta)
mixed salad
ensaladilla rusa
Russian salad
escalope
escalope
espárragos
asparagus
especies
spices
espinaca
spinach
fideos
noodles
filete
fillet
flan
cream caramel
frambuesa
raspberry
fresa
strawberry
frito
fried
fruta (del tiempo)
seasonal fruit

galleta
biscuit
gambas
prawns
garbanzos
chick peas
gazpacho andaluz
gazpacho (cold soup)
granizado de limón/café
iced drink (lemon/coffee)
grosellas
red/black currants
guisado
stew
guisantes
peas
habas
broad beans
harina
flour
hígado de oca
goose liver
higo
fig
huevos al plato/ duros/revueltos
fried/hard boiled/scrambled eggs

jamón de York/serrano
ham (cooked/Parma style)
jerez (seco, dulce)
sherry (dry, sweet)
judías verdes
French beans
jugo/zumo
fruit juice
langosta
lobster
langostino
crayfish
leche
milk
lechuga
lettuce
legumbres
vegetables (legumes)
lengua
tongue
lenguado
sole
lentejas
lentils
licor
liqueur
liebre
hare
limón
lemon
lomo de cerdo
tenderloin of pork

maíz (mazorca)
corn (on the cob)
mantequilla
butter
manzana
apple
mazapán
marzipan
mejillones
mussels
melocotón (en almíbar)
peach (in syrup)
melón
melon
membrillo
quince
merluza
hake
mermelada
jam
mero
sea bass
morcilla
black pudding
mostaza
mustard
muslo de pollo
drumstick
nuez
walnut
ostras
oysters
paella
paella

pan
bread
pastel
cake
patatas fritas
chips/crisps
pato (silvestre)
(wild) duck
pechuga (de pollo)
(chicken) breast
pepino
cucumber
pepinillos
gherkins
pera
pear
perdiz
partridge
perejil
parsley
pescado
fish
picadillo de ternera
minced veal
pierna (de cordero)
leg (of lamb)
pimentón
paprika
pimienta
pepper
pimientos
green/red peppers
piña
pineapple

plancha (a la)
grilled
plátano
banana
plato principal
main course
platos típicos
regional specialities
pollo
chicken
puerro
leek
pulpo
octopus
queso
cheese
rábanos
radishes
rabo de buey
oxtail
rape
monkfish
remolacha
beetroot
riñones
kidneys
rodaballo
turbot
romana (a la)
deep fried
vino rosado
rosé wine
salchicha
sausage
salchichón
salami
salmón
salmon
salmón ahumado
smoked salmon
salmonete
red mullet
sandía
water melon
sangría
sangría
sardinas
sardines
setas
mushrooms
solomillo de buey
fillet of beef
sopa
soup
tarta helada
ice cream cake
ternera
veal
tinto
red wine
tocino
bacon
tortilla española
Spanish omelette (potato)
tortilla francesa
plain omelette
tortitas
waffles
trucha
trout
trufas
truffles
turrón
nougat
uvas
grapes
verduras
green vegetables
vinagre
vinegar
zanahorias
carrots
zumo de naranja
orange juice

5

On the road

5.1 Asking for directions

Excuse me, could I ask you something?	Perdone, ¿podría preguntarle algo? *pehrdohneh, pohdreeah prehgoontahrleh ahlgoh?*
I've lost my way	Me he perdido *meh eh pehrdeedoh*
Is there a(n)... around here?	¿Sabe dónde hay un(a)...por aquí? *sahbeh dohndeh ay oon(ah)...pohr ahkee?*
Is this the way to...?	¿Se va por aquí a...? *seh bah pohr ahkee ah...?*
Could you tell me how to get to the... (name of place) by car/on foot?	¿Podría decirme cómo llegar a... (en coche/a pie)? *pohdreeah dehtheermeh kohmoh lyehgahr ah... (ehn kohcheh/ah pyeh)?*
What's the quickest way to...?	¿Cómo hago para llegar lo antes posible a...? *kohmoh ahgoh pahrah lyehgahr loh ahntehs pohseebleh ah...?*
How many kilometres is it to...?	¿Cuántos kilómetros faltan para llegar a...? *kwahntohs keelohmehtrohs fahltahn pahrah lyehgahr ah...?*
Could you point it out on the map?	¿Podría señalarlo en el mapa? *pohdreeah sehnyahlahrloh ehn ehl mahpah?*

No sé; no soy de aquí	I don't know, I don't know my way around here
Por aquí no es	You're going the wrong way
Tiene que volver a...	You have to go back to...
Allí los carteles le indicarán	From there on just follow the signs
Vuelva a preguntar allí	When you get there, ask again

todo recto	la calle	el viaducto
straight ahead	the street	the fly-over
a la izquierda	el semáforo	el puente
left	the traffic light	the bridge
a la derecha	el túnel	el paso a nivel/las barreras
right	the tunnel	the level crossing/the boom gates
doblar	el stop	el cartel en dirección de...
turn	the `give way' sign	the sign pointing to...
seguir	el edificio	la flecha
follow	the building	the arrow
cruzar	en la esquina	
cross	at the corner	
el cruce	el río	
the intersection	the river	

5.2 Customs

● **Border documents:** along with your passport you must carry your original valid full driving licence (together with paper counterpart if photocard licence), vehicle registration document and motor insurance certificate. Contact your motor insurer for advice at least a month before taking your vehicle overseas to ensure that you are covered. There is no restriction, either by quantity or value, on goods purchased by travellers from another EU country provided they are for their own personal use. Guidelines have been published. As these are subject to change you are advised to contact your travel agent, customs or the Embassy for further details before travelling.

My children are entered on this passport	**Mis hijos están apuntados en este pasaporte** *mees eehohs ehstahn ahpoontahdohs ehn ehsteh pahsahpohrteh*
I'm travelling through___	**Estoy de paso** *ehstoy deh pahsoh*

Su pasaporte, por favor	Your passport, please
La tarjeta verde, por favor	Your green card, please
El permiso de circulación/la carta gris, por favor	Your vehicle documents, please
¿Adónde va?	Where are you heading?
¿Cuánto tiempo piensa quedarse?	How long are you planning to stay?
¿Tiene algo que declarar?	Do you have anything to declare?
¿Puede abrir esto?	Open this, please

I'm going on holiday to...	Voy de vacaciones a... *boy deh bahkahthyohnehs ah...*
I'm on a business trip	He venido en viaje de negocios *eh behneedoh ehn byahheh deh nehgohthyohs*
I don't know how long I'll be staying yet	Todavía no sé cuánto tiempo me quedaré *tohdahbeeah noh seh kwahntoh tyehmpoh meh kehdahreh*
I'll be staying here for a weekend	Pienso quedarme un fin de semana *pyehnsoh kehdahrmeh oon feen deh sehmahnah*
– for a few days	Pienso quedarme unos días *pyehnsoh kehdahrmeh oonohs deeahs*
– for a week	Pienso quedarme una semana *pyehnsoh kehdahrmeh oonah sehmahnah*
– for two weeks	Pienso quedarme dos semanas *pyehnsoh kehdahrmeh dohs sehmahnahs*
I've got nothing to declare	No tengo nada que declarar *noh tehngoh nahdah keh dehklahrahr*
I've got...with me	Traigo... *trahygoh...*

– ...cartons of cigarettes	Traigo...cartones de cigarrillos *trahygoh...kahrtohnehs deh theegahrreelyohs*
– ...bottles of...	Traigo...botellas de... *trahygoh...bohtehlyahs deh...*
– some souvenirs	Traigo algunos recuerdos de viaje *trahygoh ahlgoonohs rehkwehrdohs de byahheh*
These are personal effects	Estos son artículos personales *ehstohs sohn ahrteekoolohs pehrsohnahlehs*
These are not new	Estas cosas no son nuevas *ehstahs kohsahs noh sohn nwehbahs*
Here's the receipt	Aquí está el recibo *ahkee ehstah ehl rehtheeboh*
This is for private use	Esto es para uso personal *ehstoh ehs pahrah oosoh pehrsohnahl*
How much import duty do I have to pay?	¿Cuánto tengo que pagar por derechos de aduana? *kwahntoh tehngoh keh pahgahr pohr dehrehchohs deh ahdwahnah?*
Can I go now?	¿Puedo seguir? *pwehdoh sehgheer?*

5.3 Luggage

Porter!	¡Mozo! *mohthoh!*
Could you take this luggage to...?	¿Podría llevar este equipaje a...? *pohdreeah lyehbahr ehsteh ehkeepahheh ah...?*
How much do I owe you?	¿Cuánto le debo? *kwahntoh leh dehboh?*

Where can I find a luggage trolley?	¿Dónde hay carritos para el equipaje? *dohndeh ay kahrreetohs pahrah ehl ehkeepahheh?*
Could you store this luggage for me?	¿Podría dejar este equipaje en la consigna? *pohdreeah dehhahr ehsteh ehkeepahheh ehn lah kohnseegnah?*
Where are the luggage lockers?	¿Dónde está la consigna automática? *dohndeh ehstah lah kohnseegnah ahootohmahteekah?*
I can't get the locker open	No logro abrir la puerta de la consigna *noh lohgroh ahbreer lah pwehrtah deh lah kohnseegnah*
How much is it per item per day?	¿Cuánto sale por bulto y por día? *kwahntoh sahleh pohr booltoh ee pohr deeah?*
This is not my bag/suitcase	Este/ésta no es mi bolso/mi maleta *ehsteh/ehstah noh ehs mee bohlsoh/mee mahlehtah*
There's one item/bag/suitcase missing still	Todavía falta un bulto/un bolso/una maleta *tohdahbeeah fahltah oon booltoh/oon bohlsoh/oonah mahlehtah*
My suitcase is damaged	Me han dañado la maleta *meh ahn dahnyahdoh lah mahlehtah*

The parts of a car

battery	la batería	*lah bahtehreeah*
rear light	el faropiloto	*ehl fahroh peelohtoh*
rear-view mirror	el retrovisor	*ehl rehtrohbeesohr*
reversing light	la luz de marcha atrás	*lah looth deh mahrchah ahtrahs*
aerial	la antena	*lah ahntehnah*
car radio	la autorradio	*lah ahootohrrahdyoh*
petrol tank	el depósito de gasolina	*ehl dehpohseetoh deh gahsohleenah*
inside mirror	el espejo interior	*ehl ehspehhoh eentehreeohr*
sparking plugs	las bujías	*lahs booheeahs*
fuel filter/pump	el separador de gasolina	*ehl sehpahrahdohr deh gahsohleenah*
wing mirror	el espejo exterior	*ehl ehspehoh ehxtehryohr*
bumper	el parachoques	*ehl pahrahchohkehs*
carburettor	el carburador	*ehl kahrboorahdohr*
crankcase	el cárter	*ehl kahrtehr*
cylinder	el cilindro	*ehl theeleendroh*
ignition	los contactos del ruptor	*lohs kohntahktohs dehl rooptohr*
warning light	la luz piloto	*lah looth peelohtoh*
dynamo	la dinamo	*lah deenahmoh*
accelerator	el pedal del acelerador	*ehl pehdahl dehl ahthehlehrahdohr*
handbrake	el freno de mano	*ehl frehnoh deh mahnoh*
valve	la válvula	*lah bahlboolah*
silencer	el silenciador	*ehl seelehnthyahdohr*
boot	el maletero	*ehl mahlehtehroh*
headlight	el faro	*ehl fahroh*
crank shaft	el cigueñal	*ehl theegwehnyahl*
air filter	el filtro de aire	*ehl feeltroh deh ayreh*
fog lamp	la luz antiniebla trasera	*llah looth ahnteenyehblah trahsehrah*
engine block	el bloque motor	*ehl blohkeh mohtohr*

camshaft	el árbol de levas	*ehl ahrbohl deh lehbahs*
oil filter/pump	el filtro de aceitela	*ehl feeltroh deh ahtheheeteh*
dipstick	la varilla indicadora de nivel de aceite	*lah bahreelyah eendeekahdohrah deh neebehl deh ahtheyteh*
pedal	el pedal	*ehl pehdahl*
door	la portezuela	*lah pohrtehthwehlah*
radiator	el radiador	*ehl rahdyahdohr*
brake disc	el disco del freno	*ehl deeskoh dehl frehnoh*
spare wheel	la rueda de reserva	*lah rwehdah deh rehsehrbah*
indicator	el intermitente	*ehl eentehrmeetehnteh*
steering wheel	el volante	*ehl bohlahnteh*
windscreen wiper	el limpiaparabrisas	*ehl leempyahpahrahbreesahs*
shock absorbers	los amortiguadores	*lohs ahmohrteegwahdohrehs*
sunroof	el techo corredizo	*ehl tehchoh kohrrehdeethoh*
spoiler	el spoiler	*ehl spoheelehr*
starter motor	el motor de arranque	*ehl mohtohr deh ahrrahnkeh*
steering column	el cárter de la dirección	*ehl kahrtehr deh lah deerehkthyohn*
exhaust pipe	el tubo de escape	*ehl tooboh deh ehskahpeh*
seat belt	el cinturón de seguridad	*ehl theentoorohn deh sehgooreedahdh*
fan	el ventilador	*ehl behnteelahdohr*
distributor cables	los cables del distribuidor	*lohs kahblehs dehl deestreebweedohr*
gear lever	la palanca de cambios	*lah pahlahnkah deh kahmbyohs*
windscreen	el parabrisas	*ehl pahrahbreesahs*
water pump	la bomba de agua	*lah bohmbah deh ahgwah*
wheel	la rueda	*lah rwehdah*
hubcap	el tapacubos	*ehl tahpahkoobohs*
piston	el émbolo	*ehl ehmbohloh*

5.4 Traffic signs

a la derecha
right
a la izquierda
left
abierto
open
altura máxima
maximum height
arcenes sin afirmar
soft verges
¡atención, peligro!
danger
autopista de peaje
toll road
autovía
motorway
bajada peligrosa
steep hill
calzada resbaladiza
slippery road
cambio de sentido
change of direction
cañada
animals crossing
carretera comarcal
secondary road
carretera cortada
road closed
carretera en mal estado
irregular road surface
carretera nacional
main road
ceda el paso
give way
cerrado
closed
cruce peligroso
dangerous crossing
curvas en ... km
bends for...km
despacio
drive slowly
desprendimientos
loose rocks
desvío
diversion
dirección prohibida
no entry
dirección única
one-way traffic
encender las luces
switch on lights
espere
wait
estacionamiento reglamentado
limited parking zone
excepto...
except for...
fin de...
end of...
hielo
ice on road
niebla
beware fog
obras
roadworks ahead
paso a nivel (sin barreras)
level crossing (no gates)
paso de ganado
cattle crossing
peaje
toll
peatones
pedestrian crossing
precaución
caution
prohibido aparcar
no parking
prohibido adelantar
no overtaking
puesto de socorro
first aid
salida
exit
salida de camiones
factory/works exit
substancias peligrosas
dangerous substances
travesía peligrosa
dangerous crossing
zona peatonal
pedestrian zone

5.5 The car

● **The motorways** in Spain have been very well updated and expanded. Tolls, however, can be expensive.
Particular traffic regulations:
maximum speed for cars:
120km/h on toll roads, 110km/h on other motorways, 90km/h outside built-up areas, 50km/h in built-up areas
– give way: all traffic from the right has the right of way, except for major roads and thoroughfares.

It is compulsory to carry a spare set of bulbs and a warning triangle. Drivers and/or passengers must wear a reflective jacket when exiting a car which has broken down on a motorway or main or busy road.

5.6 The petrol station

● **Petrol is easily available** but rather expensive in Spain.

How many kilometres to the next petrol station, please?	**¿Cuántos kilómetros faltan para la próxima gasolinera?** *kwahntohs keelohmehtrohs fahltahn pahrah lah prohxeemah gahsohleenehrah?*
I would like...litres of..., please	**Póngame...litros de..., por favor** *pohngahmeh...leetrohs deh..., pohr fahbohr*
– super	**Póngame...litros de gasolina súper** *pohngahmeh...leetrohs de gahsohleenah soopehr*
– leaded	**Póngame...litros de gasolina normal** *pohngahmeh...leetrohs deh gahsohleenah nohrmahl*
– unleaded	**Póngame...litros de gasolina sin plomo** *pohngahmeh...leetrohs deh gahsohleenah seen plohmoh*

– diesel	Póngame...litros de gasóleo *pohngahmeh...leetrohs deh gahsohlehoh*
I would like...euros' worth of petrol, please	Póngame gasolina por...euros *pohngahmeh gahsohleenah pohr...euros*
Fill her up, please	Lléneme el depósito, por favor *lyehnehmeh ehl dehpohseetoh, pohr fahvohr*
Could you check...?	¿Podría controlar...? *pohdreeah kohntrohlahr?*
– the oil level	¿Podría controlar el nivel del aceite? *pohdreeah kohntrohlahr ehl neebehl dehl ahtheheeteh?*
– the tyre pressure	¿Podría controlar la presión de los neumáticos? *pohdreeah kohntrohlahr lah prehsyohn deh lohs nehoomahteekohs?*
Could you change the oil, please?	¿Podría cambiar el aceite? *pohdreeah kahmbyahr ehl atheheeteh?*
Could you clean the windows/the windscreen, please?	¿Podría limpiar los cristales/el parabrisas? *pohdreeah leempyahr lohs kreestahlehs/ehl pahrahbreesahs?*
Could you give the car a wash, please?	¿Podría lavar el coche? *pohdreeah lahbahr ehl kohcheh?*

5.7 Breakdown and repairs

I'm having car trouble. Could you give me a hand?	Tengo una avería. ¿Podría ayudarme? *tehngoh oonah ahbehreeah. pohdreeah ahyoodahrmeh?*
I've run out of petrol	Me he quedado sin gasolina *meh eh kehdahdoh seen gahsohleenah*

I've locked the keys in the car	Me he dejado las llaves en el coche *meh eh dehhahdoh lahs lyabehs ehn ehl kohcheh*
The car/motorbike/ moped won't start	El coche/la moto/el ciclomotor no arranca *ehl kohcheh/lah mohtoh/ehl theeklohmohtohr noh ahrrahnkah*
Could you contact the recovery service for me, please?	¿Podría avisar al auxilio en carretera? *pohdreeah ahbeesar ahl ahooxeelyoh ehn kahrrehtehrah?*
Could you call a garage for me, please?	¿Podría llamar por teléfono a un taller mecánico? *pohdreeah lyahmahr pohr tehlehfohnoh ah oon tahlyehr mehkahneekoh?*
Could you give me a lift to...?	¿Me podría llevar a...? *meh pohdreeah lyehbahr ah...?*
– a garage/into town?	¿Me podría llevar a un taller mecánico/a la ciudad? *meh pohdreeah lyehbahr ah oon tahlyehr mehkahneekoh/ah lah thyoodahdh?*
– a phone booth?	¿Me podría llevar a una cabina de teléfonos? *meh pohdreeah lyehbahr ah oonah kahbeenah deh tehlehfohnohs?*
– an emergency phone?	¿Me podría llevar a un teléfono de emergencia? *meh pohdreeah lyehbahr ah oon tehlehfohnoh deh ehmehrhehnthyah?*
Can we take my bicycle/moped?	¿Podríamos llevar la bicicleta/el ciclomotor? *pohdreeahmohs lyehbahr lah beetheeklehtah/ehl theeklohmohtohr?*
Could you tow me to a garage?	¿Podría remolcarme hasta un taller mecánico? *pohdreeah rehmohlkahrmeh ahstah oon tahlyehr mehkahneekoh?*

There's probably something wrong with...(See 5.8).	**Me parece que está fallando el/la...** *meh pahrehtheh keh ehstah fahlyahndoh ehl/lah...*
Can you fix it?	**¿Podría arreglarlo?** *pohdreeah ahrrehglahrloh?*
Could you fix my tyre?	**¿Podría arreglar el neumático?** *pohdreeah ahrrehglahr ehl nehoomahteekoh?*
Could you change this wheel?	**¿Podría cambiar esta rueda?** *pohdreeah kahmbyahr ehstah rwehdah?*
Can you fix it so it'll get me to...?	**¿Podría arreglarlo de tal manera que pueda seguir hasta...?** *pohdreeah ahrrehglahrloh deh tahl mahnehrah keh pwehdah sehgheer ahstah...?*
Which garage can help me?	**¿En qué taller me podrán ayudar entonces?** *ehn keh tahlyehr meh pohdrahn ahyoodahr ehntohnthehs?*
When will my car/bicycle be ready?	**¿Para cuándo estará mi coche/bicicleta?** *pahrah kwahndoh ehstahrah mee kohcheh/beetheeklehtah?*
Can I wait for it here?	**¿Puedo esperar aquí?** *pwehdoh ehspehrahr ahkee?*
How much will it cost?	**¿Por cuánto me va a salir?** *pohr kwahntoh meh bah ah sahleer?*
Could you itemise the bill?	**¿Podría especificar la cuenta?** *pohdreeah ehspehtheefeekahr lah kwehntah?*
Can I have a receipt for the insurance?	**¿Me podría dar un recibo para el seguro?** *meh pohdreeah dahr oon rehtheeboh pahrah ehl sehgooroh?*

5.8 The bicycle/moped

● **Cycle paths** are rare in Spain. Not much consideration for bikes should be expected on the roads. The maximum speed for mopeds is 40km/h both inside and outside town centres. A helmet is compulsory.

No tengo piezas de recambio para su coche/su bicicleta	I don't have parts for your car/bicycle
Las piezas de recambio me las tienen que traer de otro sitio	I have to get the parts from somewhere else
Las piezas de recambio tengo que encargarlas	I have to order the parts
Eso llevará medio día	That'll take half a day
Eso llevará un día	That'll take a day
Eso llevará unos días	That'll take a few days
Eso llevará una semana	That'll take a week
Su coche ha quedado totalmente destruido	Your car is a write-off
Ya no se puede hacer nada para arreglarlo	It can't be repaired.
El coche/la moto/el ciclomotor/la bicicleta estará para las...	The car/motor bike/moped/bicycle will be ready at... o'clock.

The parts of a bicycle

rear lamp	el piloto	*ehl peelohtoh*
rear wheel	la rueda trasera	*lah rwehdah trahsehrah*
(luggage) carrier	el portaequipajes	*ehl pohrtahehkeepahhehs*
bicycle fork	la cabeza	*lah kahbehthah*
bell	el timbre	*ehl teembreh*
inner tube	la cámara	*lah kahmahrah*
tyre	el neumático/la cubierta	*ehl nehoomahteekoh/lah koobyehrtah*
crank	la biela	*lah byehlah*
gear change	el cambio de velocidades	*ehl kahmbyoh deh behlotheedahdehs*
wire	el hilo	*ehl eeloh*
dynamo	la dinamo	*lah deenahmoh*
bicycle trailer	el remolque de bicicleta	*ehl rehmohlkeh deh beetheeklehtah*
frame	el cuadro	*ehl kwahdroh*
dress guard	el guardafaldas	*ehl gwardahfahldahs*
chain	la cadena de rodillos	*lah kahdehnah deh rohdeelyohs*
chain guard	el cubrecadena/el cárter	*ehl koobrehkahdehnah/ehl kahrtehr*
chain lock	la cadena antirrobo	*lah kahdehnah ahnteerrohboh*
milometer	el contador kilométrico	*ehl kohntahdohr keelohmehtreekoh*
child's seat	el sillín para niños	*ehl seelyeen pahrah neenyohs*
headlamp	el faro	*ehl fahroh*
bulb	la bombilla	*lah bohmbeelyah*
pedal	el pedal	*ehl pehdahl*
pump	la bombilla	*lah bohmbeelyah*
reflector	el cristal reflectante	*ehl kreestahl rehflehktahnteh*

brake pad	la zapatilla del freno	*lah thahpahteelyah dehl frehnoh*
brake cable	el cable del freno	*ehl kahbleh dehl frehnoh*
ring lock	la cerradura	*lah thehrrahdoorah*
carrier straps	las bandas elásticas	*lahs bahndahs ehlahsteekahs*
spoke	el radio/el rayo	*ehl rahdyoh/ehl rahyoh*
mudguard	el guardabarros	*ehl gwahrdahbahrrohs*
handlebar	el manillar	*ehl mahneelyahr*
chain wheel	el piñón	*ehl peenyohn*
toe clip	el calapiés	*ehl kahlahpyehs*
crank axle	el eje del cigueñal	*ehl ehheh dehl theegwehnyal*
drum brake	el freno de tambor	*ehl frehnoh deh tahmbohr*
tube	la llanta	*lah lyahntah*
valve	la válvula	*lah bahlboolah*
valve tube	el tubo de la válvula	*ehl tooboh deh lah bahlboolah*
gear cable	el cable de velocidades	*ehl kahbleh deh behlohtheedahdehs*
fork	la horquilla	*lah ohrkeelyah*
front wheel	la rueda delantera	*lah rwehdah dehlahntehrah*
seat	el sillín	*el seelyeen*

5.9 Renting a vehicle

I'd like to rent a...	Quisiera alquilar un... *keesyehrah ahlkeelahr oon...*
Do I need a (special) licence for that?	¿Hace falta un permiso de conducir (especial)? *ahtheh fahltah oon pehrmeesoh deh kohndootheer (ehspehthyahl)?*
I'd like to rent the...for...	Quisiera alquilar el/la...por... *keesyehrah ahlkeelahr ehl/lah...pohr...*
– one day	Quisiera alquilar el/la...por un día *keesyehrah ahlkeelahr ehl/lah...pohr oon deeah*
– two days	Quisiera alquilar el/la...por dos días *keesyehrah ahlkeelahr ehl/lah...pohr dohs deeahs*
How much is that per day/week?	¿Cuánto sale por día/semana? *kwahntoh sahleh pohr deeah/pohr sehmahnah?*
How much is the deposit?	¿Cuánto es la fianza? *kwahntoh ehs lah fyahnthah?*
Could I have a receipt for the deposit?	¿Me podría dar un recibo por el pago de la fianza? *meh pohdreeah dahr oon rehtheeboh pohr ehl pahgoh deh lah fyahnthah?*
How much is the surcharge per kilometre?	¿Cuánto hay que pagar extra por kilómetro? *kwahntoh ay keh pahgahr ehxtrah pohr keelohmehtroh?*
Does that include petrol?	¿Está incluida la gasolina? *ehstah eenklooeedah lah gahsohleenah?*
Does that include insurance?	¿Está incluido el seguro? *ehstah eenklooeedoh ehl sehgooroh?*

What time can I pick the...up tomorrow?	¿A qué hora puedo pasar mañana a buscar el/la...? *ah keh ohrah pwehdoh pahsahr mahnyahnah ah booskahr ehl/lah...?*
When does the...have to be back?	¿A qué hora tengo que devolver el/la...? *ah keh ohrah tehngoh keh dehbohlbehr ehl/lah...?*
Where's the petrol tank?	¿Dónde está el depósito de gasolina? *dohndeh ehstah ehl dehpohseetoh deh gahsohleenah?*
What sort of fuel does it take?	¿Qué tipo de combustible hay que echarle? *keh teepoh deh kohmboosteebleh ay keh ehchahrleh?*

5.10 Hitchhiking

Where are you heading?	¿Adónde va? *ahdohndeh bah?*
Can I come along?	¿Me podría llevar? *meh pohdreeah lyehbahr?*
Can my boyfriend/girlfriend come too?	¿Podría llevar también a mi amigo/amiga? *pohdreeah lyehbahr tahmbyehn ah mee ahmeegoh/ahmeegah?*
I'm trying to get to...	Voy a... *boy ah...*
Is that on the way to...?	¿Eso está camino de...? *ehsoh ehstah kahmeenoh deh...?*
Could you drop me off...?	¿Me podría dejar...? *meh pohdreeah dehhahr...?*
– here?	¿Me podría dejar aquí mismo? *meh pohdreeah dehhahr ahkee meesmoh?*

– at the...exit?	¿Me podría dejar en la salida de...? *meh pohdreeah dehhahr ehn lah sahleedah deh...?*
– in the centre?	¿Me podría dejar en el centro? *meh pohdreeah dehhahr ehn ehl thehntroh?*
– at the next roundabout?	¿Me podría dejar en la próxima rotonda? *meh pohdreeah dehhahr ehn lah prohxeemah rohtohndah?*
Could you stop here, please?	¿Podría pararse aquí? *pohdreeah pahrahrseh ahkee?*
I'd like to get out here	Quisiera bajarme aquí *keesyehrah bahhahrmeh ahkee*
Thanks for the lift	Gracias por llevarme *grahthyahs pohr lyehbahrmeh*

6 Public transport

6.1 In general

● **The rail network** has been substantially overhauled and expanded and there is now a good, fast service available with the Talgo and Ave in the south. These trains require payment of a supplement and it is advisable to reserve seats in advance, at the station or at travel agencies. Tickets for buses and the metro can be bought at an *estanco*, as well as metro stations.

Announcements

El tren [de las 10.40] con destino a..., ..., saldrá con (unos)...minutos de retraso	The [10.40] train to...has been delayed by 15 minutes
Por la vía 5 entrará el tren [de las 10.40] con destino a.../ procedente de...	The train now arriving at platform 5 is the [10.40] train to .../from...
En la vía 5 está por partir el tren [de las 10.40]...	The [10.40] train to...is about to leave from platform 5
Su atención, por favor Manténganse lejos de la via; un tren Intercity pasará por la plataforma...	Attention please! Keep your distance from the rail track, an intercity train will pass on platform...
Nos estamos aproximando a la estación de...	We're now approaching...

Where does this train go to?	¿Adónde va este tren? *ahdohndeh bah ehsteh trehn?*
Does this boat go to...?	¿Este barco va a...? *ehsteh bahrkoh bah ah...?*
Can I take this bus to...?	¿Puedo coger este autobús para ir a...? *pwehdoh kohhehr ehsteh ahootohboos pahrah eer ah...?*

Does this train stop at...? ___	¿Este tren para en...? *ehsteh trehn pahrah ehn...?*
Is this seat taken/free /reserved? ___	¿Está ocupado/libre/reservado este asiento? *ehstah ohkoopahdoh/leebreh/ rehsehrbahdoh ehsteh ahsyehntoh?*
I've booked... ___	He reservado... *eh rehsehrbahdoh...*
Could you tell me where I have to get off for... ? ___	¿Me podría decir dónde me tengo que bajar para ir a...? *meh pohdreeah dehtheer dohndeh meh tehngoh keh bahhar pahrah eer ah...?*
Could you let me know when we get to...? ___	¿Me podría avisar cuando lleguemos a...? *meh pohdreeah ahbeesahr kwahndoh lyehghehmohs ah...?*
Could you stop at the next stop, please? ___	La próxima parada, por favor *lah prohxeemah pahrahdah pohr fahbohr*
Where are we now? ___	¿Dónde estamos? *dohndeh ehstahmohs?*
Do I have to get off here? ___	¿Tengo que bajarme aquí? *tehngoh keh bahhahrmeh ahkee?*
Have we already passed...? ___	¿Ya hemos pasado...? *yah ehmohs pahsahdoh...?*
How long have I been asleep? ___	¿Cuánto tiempo he dormido? *kwahntoh tyehmpoh eh dohrmeedoh?*
How long does... stop here? ___	¿Cuánto tiempo se queda aquí...? *kwahntoh tyehmpoh seh kehdah ahkee?*
Can I come back on the same ticket? ___	¿Este billete me sirve para volver? *ehsteh beelyehteh meh seerbeh pahrah bohlbehr?*
Can I change on this ticket? ___	¿Se puede hacer trasbordo con este billete? *seh pwehdeh ahthehr trahsbohrdoh kohn ehsteh beelyehteh?*
How long is this ticket valid for? ___	¿Hasta cuándo es válido este billete? *ahstah kwahndoh ehs bahleedoh ehsteh beelyehteh*

How much is the ______ supplement for the Talgo/Ave (high speed train)?	¿Cuánto vale el suplemento para el Talgo/el Ave? *kwahntoh bahleh ehl sooplehmehntoh pahrah ehl tahlgoh/ehl ahbeh?*

6.2 Questions to passengers

Ticket types

¿Primera o segunda clase?	First or second class?
¿Billete de ida o de ida y vuelta?	Single or return?
¿Fumadores o no fumadores?	Smoking or non-smoking?
¿Ventanilla o pasillo?	Window or aisle?
¿Adelante o atrás?	Front or back?
¿Asiento o litera?	Seat or couchette?
¿Arriba, en el medio o abajo?	Top, middle or bottom?
¿Clase turista o preferente?	Tourist class or business class?
¿Camarote o butaca?	Cabin or seat?
¿Individual o doble?	Single or double?
¿Cuántas personas viajan?	How many are travelling?

Destination

¿Adónde quiere ir?	Where are you travelling?
¿Qué día sale?	When are you leaving?
Su...sale a las...	Your...leaves at...
Tiene que hacer trasbordo	You have to change trains
Tiene que bajarse en...	You have to get off at...
Tiene que pasar por...	You have to travel via...
El viaje de ida es el día...	The outward journey is on...
El viaje de vuelta es el día...	The return journey is on...
Tiene que embarcar a las...a más tardar	You have to be on board by...

Inside the vehicle

Billetes, por favor	Your ticket, please
Su reserva, por favor	Your reservation, please
Su pasaporte, por favor	Your passport, please
Se ha equivocado de asiento	You're in the wrong seat
Se ha equivocado de...	You're on/in the wrong...
Este asiento está reservado	This seat is reserved
Tiene que pagar un suplemento	You'll have to pay a supplement
El...tiene un retraso de...minutos	The...has been delayed by...minutes

6.3 Tickets

Where can I...?	¿Dónde...? *dohndeh...?*
– buy a ticket?	¿Dónde se compran los billetes? *dohndeh seh kohmprahn lohs beelyehtehs?*
– make a reservation?	¿Dónde se hacen las reservas? *dohndeh seh ahthehn lahs rehsehrbahs?*
– book a flight?	¿Dónde puedo hacer una reserva para un vuelo? *dohndeh pwehdoh ahthehr oonah rehsehrbah pahrah oon bwehloh?*
Could I have a...to..., please?	Quiero un/una...a... *kyehroh oon/oonah...ah...*
– a single	Quiero un billete de ida a... *kyehroh oon beelyehteh deh eedah ah...*
– a return	Quiero un billete de ida y vuelta a... *kyehroh oon beelyehteh deh eedah ee bwehltah ah...*

first class ____________ en primera clase
ehn preemehrah klahseh

second class __________ en segunda clase
ehn sehgoondah klahseh

tourist class __________ en clase turista
ehn klahseh tooreestah

business class ________ en clase preferente
ehn klahseh prehfehrehnteh

I'd like to book a seat/couchette/cabin ______ Quisiera reservar un asiento/una litera/un camarote
keesyehrah rehsehrbahr oon ahsyehntoh/oonah leetehrah/oon kahmahrohteh

I'd like to book a berth in the sleeping car _ Quisiera reservar una plaza en un coche cama
keesyehrah rehsehrbahr oonah plahthah ehn oon kohcheh kahmah

top/middle/bottom _____ arriba/en el medio/abajo
ahrreebah/ehn ehl mehdyoh/ahbahhoh

smoking/no smoking ___ fumadores/no fumadores
foomahdohrehs/noh foomahdohrehs

by the window ________ ventanilla
behntahneelyah

single/double _________ individual/doble
eendeebeedwahl/dohbleh

at the front/back _______ adelante/atrás
ahdehlahnteh/ahtrahs

There are...of us ______ Somos...personas
sohmohs...pehrsohnahs

a car __________________ un coche
oon kohcheh

a caravan _____________ una caravana
oonah kahrahbahnah

...bicycles _____________ ...bicicletas
...beetheeklehtahs

Do you also have...? ___ ¿Tienen...?
tyehnehn...?

– season tickets?	¿Tienen billetes para varios viajes? *tyehnen beelyehtehs pahrah bahryohs byahhehs?*
– weekly tickets?	¿Tienen abonos semanales? *tyehnehn ahbohnohs sehmahnahlehs?*
– monthly season tickets?	¿Tienen abonos mensuales? *tyehnehn ahbohnohs mehnswahlehs?*

6.4 Information

Where's-?	¿Dónde hay...? *dohndeh ay...?*
Where's the information desk?	¿Dónde está la oficina de información? *dohndeh ehstah lah ohfeetheenah deh eenfohrmahthyohn?*
Where can I find a timetable?	¿Dónde hay un horario? *dohndeh ay oon ohrahryoh?*
Where's the...desk?	¿Dónde está el mostrador de...? *dohndeh ehstah ehl mohstrahdohr deh...?*
Do you have a city map with the bus/the underground routes on it?	¿Tendría un plano de la ciudad con la red de autobuses/metro? *tehndreeah oon plahnoh deh lah thyoodahdh kohn lah rehth deh ahootohbooseh s/mehtroh?*
Do you have a timetable?	¿Tendría un horario? *tehndreeah oon ohrahryoh?*
I'd like to confirm/ cancel/change my booking for/trip to...	Quisiera confirmar/cancelar/cambiar mi reserva/mi viaje a... *keesyehrah kohnfeermahr/kahnthehlahr/kahmbyahr mee rehsehrbah/mee byahheh ah...*
Will I get my money back?	¿Me devuelven el dinero? *meh dehbwehlbehn ehl deenehroh?*

I want to go to... How do I get there? (What's the quickest way there?)	Tengo que ir a...¿Cómo hago para llegar (lo más rápido posible)? *tehngoh keh eer ah...kohmoh ahgoh pahrah lyehgahr(loh mahs rahpeedoh pohseebleh)?*
How much is a single/return to...?	¿Cuánto vale un billete de ida/de ida y vuelta a...? *kwahntoh bahleh oon beelyehteh deh eedah ee bwehltah ah...?*
Do I have to pay a supplement?	¿Tengo que pagar algún suplemento? *tehngoh keh pahgahr ahlgoon sooplehmehntoh?*
Can I interrupt my journey with this ticket?	¿Con este billete puedo hacer una parada intermedia? *kohn ehsteh beelyehteh pwehdoh ahthehr oonah pahrahdah eentehrmehdyah?*
How much luggage am I allowed?	¿Cuánto equipaje puedo llevar? *kwahntoh ehkeepahheh pwehdoh lyebahr?*
Can I send my luggage in advance?	¿Puedo enviar mi equipaje por anticipado? *pwehdoh ehnbeeahr mee ehkeepahheh pohr ahnteetheepahdoh?*
Does this...travel direct?	¿Este...va directo? *ehsteh...bah deerehktoh?*
Do I have to change? Where?	¿Tengo que hacer trasbordo? ¿Dónde? *tehngoh keh ahthehr trahsbohrdoh? dohndeh?*
Will there be any stopovers?	¿Habrá escalas? *ahbrah ehskahlahs?*
Does the boat call in at any ports on the way?	¿El barco hace alguna escala? *ehl bahrkoh ahtheh ahlgoonah ehskahlah?*
Does the train/ bus stop at...?	¿Este tren/este autobús para en...? *ehsteh trehn/ehsteh ahootohboos pahrah ehn...?*
Where should I get off?	¿Dónde me tengo que bajar? *dohndeh meh tehngoh keh bahhahr?*

Is there a connection to...?	¿Hay enlace para...? *ay ehnlahtheh pahrah...?*
How long do I have to wait?	¿Cuánto tengo que esperar? *kwahntoh tehngoh keh ehspehrahr?*
When does...leave?	¿Cuándo sale...? *kwahndoh sahleh...?*
What time does the first/next/last...leave?	¿A qué hora sale el primer/próximo/último...? *ah keh ohrah sahleh ehl preemehr/prohxeemoh/oolteemoh...?*
How long does...take?	¿Cuánto tarda...en llegar? *kwahntoh tahrdah...ehn lyehgahr?*
What time does...arrive in...?	¿A qué hora llega...a...? *ah keh ohrah lyegah...ah...?*
Where does the...to... leave from?	¿De dónde sale el...a...? *deh dohndeh sahleh ehl...ah...?*
Is this...to...?	¿Este es...a...? *ehsteh ehs...ah...?*

6.5 Aeroplanes

● **On arrival** at a Spanish airport, you will find the following signs:

llegadas arrivals	salidas departures

6.6 Trains

● **The rail network** is very extensive, run by the RENFE (Red Nacional de Ferrocarriles Españoles). Some local trains are still rather slow so it is preferable to stipulate Talgo or Rápido when buying tickets. During the summer and before public holidays it is advisable to buy train tickets well in advance. Porters are few and far between.

6.7 Taxis

● **There are plenty of taxis** in most cities. Supplements are payable for luggage and travel to stations or airports. It is advisable to inquire about the price in advance and make sure that you are hiring a city taxi.

libre	ocupado	parada de taxis
for hire	booked	taxi rank

Taxi!	¡Taxi! *tahxee!*
Could you get me a taxi, please?	¿Me podría llamar un taxi? *meh pohdreeah lyahmahr oon tahksee?*
Where can I find a taxi around here?	¿Dónde se puede coger un taxi por aquí? *dohndeh seh pwehdeh kohhehr oon tahxee pohr ahkee?*
Could you take me to..., please?	A..., por favor *ah..., pohr fahbohr*
– this address	A esta dirección, por favor *ah ehstah deerehkthyohn, pohr fahbohr*
– the...hotel	Al hotel..., por favor *ahl ohtehl..., pohr fahbohr*
– the town/city centre	Al centro, por favor *ahl thehntroh, pohr fahbohr*
– the station	A la estación, por favor *ah lah ehstahthyohn, pohr fahbohr*
– the airport	Al aeropuerto, por favor *ahl ahehrohpwehrtoh, pohr fahbohr*
How much is the trip to...?	¿Cuánto sale el recorrido hasta...? *kwahntoh sahleh ehl rehkohrreedoh ahstah...?*
How far is it to...?	¿Cuánto es hasta...? *kwahntoh ehs ahstah...?*

Could you turn on the meter, please?	¿Podría poner en marcha el taxímetro? *pohdreeah pohnehr ehn mahrchah ehl tahxeemehtroh?*
I'm in a hurry	Llevo prisa *lyehboh preesah*
Could you speed up/slow down a little?	¿Podría ir más rápido/más despacio? *pohdreeah eer mahs rahpeedoh/mahs dehspathyoh?*
Could you take a different route?	¿Podría ir por otro camino? *pohdreeah eer pohr ohtroh kahmeenoh?*
I'd like to get out here, please	Déjeme aquí *dehhehmeh ahkee*
You have to go...here	Siga...aquí *seegah...ahkee*
You have to go straight on here	Siga todo recto aquí *seegah tohdoh rehktoh akee*
You have to turn left here	Doble a la izquierda aquí *dohbleh ah lah eethkyehrdah ahkee*
You have to turn right here	Doble a la derecha aquí *dohbleh ah lah dehrehchah ahkee*
This is it	Es aquí *ehs ahkee*
Could you wait a minute for me, please?	Espéreme un momentito, por favor *ehspehrehmeh oon mohmehnteetoh, pohr fahbohr*

7 Overnight accomodation

7.1 General

● **There is great variety** in overnight accommodation in Spain. It is advisable to book (and send confirmation) in advance.

Hotel: stars indicate the degree of comfort; from five stars, the most luxurious, to one star, very basic. Most hotels offer *pensión completa* (full board) or *media pensión* (half board).

Parador: Mainly, but not always, luxurious hotels in converted castles or palaces in exceptional areas. These are very popular and have to be booked very well in advance, but are well worth the visit. They are under government supervision.

Hostal: Family run businesses for the most part, with one to three stars. They do not always provide breakfast, but are clean and can be very well situated.

Albergue: usually country inns.

Albergue de juventud: restricted to members of the international Youth Hostels Association.

Camping: a list of sites can be found at any Tourist Office.

¿Cuánto tiempo piensa quedarse?	How long will you be staying?
Rellene este formulario, por favor	Fill in this form, please
¿Me permite su pasaporte?	Could I see your passport?
Tiene que pagar una fianza	I'll need a deposit
Tiene que pagar por adelantado	You'll have to pay in advance

My name's...I've made_ a reservation over the phone/by mail — Me llamo...He reservado una habitación por teléfono/por carta
meh lyahmoh...eh rehsehrbahdoh oonah ahbeetahthyohn pohr tehlehfohnoh/pohr kahrtah

How much is it per night/week/ month? ____ ¿Cuánto sale por noche/semana/mes?
kwahntoh sahleh pohr nohcheh/sehmahnah/mehs?

We'll be staying at least...nights/weeks ____ Pensamos quedarnos al menos...noches/semanas
pehnsahmohs kehdahrnohs ahl mehnohs...nohchehs/sehmahnahs

We don't know yet ____ Todavía no lo sabemos exactamente
tohdahbeeah noh loh sahbehmohs ehxahktahmehnteh

Do you allow pets (cats/dogs)? ____ ¿Están permitidos los animales domésticos (perros/gatos)?
ehstahn pehrmeeteedohs lohs ahneemahlehs dohmehsteekohs(pehrrohs/gahtohs)?

What time does the gate/door open/close? ____ ¿A qué hora cierran/abren la verja/la puerta de entrada?
ah keh ohrah thyehrrahn/ahbrehn lah behrhah/lah pwehrtah deh ehntrahdah?

Could you get me a taxi, please? ____ ¿Podría llamar un taxi?
pohdreeah lyahmahr oon tahxee?

Is there any mail for me? ____ ¿Hay carta para mí?
ay kahrtah pahrah mee?

7.2 Camping

Where's the manager? _ ¿Dónde está el encargado?
dohndeh ehstah ehl ehnkahrgahdoh?

Are we allowed to camp here? ____ ¿Podemos acampar aquí?
pohdehmohs ahkahmpahr ahkee?

There are...of us and ...tents ____ Somos...personas y...tiendas
sohmohs...pehrsohnahs ee...tyehndahs

Puede elegir el sitio usted mismo	You can pick your own site
El sitio se lo asignamos nosotros	You'll be allocated a site
Este es el número de su emplazamiento	This is your site number
Por favor pegue esto en el parabrisas del coche	Stick this on your car, please
No pierda esta tarjeta	Please don't lose this card

Can we pick our own site? ______ ¿Podemos elegir el sitio nosotros mismos?
pohdehmohs ehlehheer ehl seetyoh nohsohtrohs meesmohs?

Do you have a quiet spot for us? ___ ¿Nos podría dar un sitio tranquilo?
nohs pohdreeah dahr oon seetyoh trahnkeeloh?

Do you have any other sites available? _ ¿No tiene otro sitio libre?
noh tyehneh ohtroh seetyoh leebreh?

It's too windy/sunny/shady here. ___ Hay mucho viento/mucho sol/mucha sombra
ay moochoh byehntoh/moochoh sohl/moochah sohmbrah

It's too crowded here _ Hay mucha gente
ay moochah hehnteh

The ground's too hard/uneven ______ El suelo es muy duro/muy desigual
ehl swehloh ehs mwee dooroh/mwee dehseegwahl

Do you have a level spot for the camper/caravan/folding caravan? ____ ¿Tiene un sitio plano para el autocaravana/la caravana/el remolque tienda?
tyehneh oon seetyoh plahnoh pahrah ehl ahootohkahrahbahnah/lah kahrahbahnah/ehl rehmohlkeh-tyehndah?

Camping equipment

luggage space	el compartimiento de equipaje	*ehl kohmpahrteemyehntoh de ehkeepahheh*
can opener	el abrelatas	*ehl ahbrehlahtahs*
butane gas bottle	la bombona (de gas butano)	*lah bohmbohnah (deh gahs bootahnoh)*
pannier	la ciclobolsa	*lah theeklohbohlsah*
gas cooker	el hornillo de gas	*ehl ohrneelyoh deh gahs*
groundsheet	la lona del suelo	*lah lohnah dehl swehloh*
mallet	el martillo	*ehl mahrteelyoh*
hammock	la hamaca	*lah ahmahkah*
jerry can	el bidón	*ehl beedohn*
campfire	la fogata	*lah fohgahtah*
folding chair	la silla plegable	*lah seelyah plehgahbleh*
insulated picnic box	la nevera portátil/la bolsa nevera	*lah nehbehrah pohrtahteel/ lah bohlsah nehbehrah*
ice pack	el acumulador	*ehl akoomoolahdohr*
compass	la brújula	*lah broohoolah*
wick	la mecha	*lah mehchah*
corkscrew	el sacacorchos	*ehl sahkahkohrchohs*
airbed	el colchón neumático	*ehl kohlchohn nehoomahteekoh*
airbed plug	el taponcito de la válvula del colchón	*ehl tahpohntheetoh deh lah bahlboolah dehl kohlchohn*
pump	la bomba neumática	*lah bohmbah nehoomahteekah*
awning	el tejadillo	*ehl tehhahdeelyoh*

Could we have adjoining sites? ¿Tiene dos plazas juntas?
tyehneh dohs plahthahs hoontahs?

Can we park the car next to the tent? ¿Podemos aparcar el coche junto a la tienda?
pohdehmohs ahpahrkahr ehl kohcheh hoontoh ah lah tyehndah?

karimat	la esterilla	*lah ehstehreelyah*
pan	la olla	*lah ohlyah*
pan handle	el mango de la olla	*ehl mahngoh deh lah ohlyah*
primus stove	el hornillo de querosén	*ehl ohrneelyoh deh kehrohsehn*
zip	la cremallera	*lah krehmalyehrah*
backpack	la mochila	*lah mohcheelah*
guy rope	el viento	*ehl byehntoh*
sleeping bag	el saco de dormir	*ehl sahkoh deh dohrmeer*
storm lantern	el farol de tormentas	*ehl fahrohl deh tohrmehntahs*
camp bed	el catre (de tijera)	*ehl kahtreh (deh teehehrah)*
table	la mesa	*lah mehsah*
tent	la tienda	*lah tyehndah*
tent peg	la estaca	*lah ehstakah*
tent pole	el palo de tienda	*ehl pahloh deh tyehndah*
vacuum flask	el termo	*ehl tehrmoh*
water bottle	la cantimplora	*lah kahnteemplohrah*
clothes peg	la pinza	*lah peenthah*
clothes line	la cuerda de tender ropa	*lah kwehrdah deh tehndehr rohpah*
windbreak	el paravientos/el paraván	*ehl pahrahbyehntohs/ehl pahrahbahn*
torch	la linterna de bolsillo	*lah leentehrnah deh bohlseelyoh*
pocket knife	la navaja	*lah nahbahhah*

How much is it per ____ person/tent/caravan/car?
¿Cuánto sale por persona/tienda/caravana/coche?
kwahntoh sahleh pohr pehrsohnah/tyehndah/kahrahbahnah/kohcheh?

Are there any...?	**¿Hay...?** *ay...?*
– any hot showers?	**¿Hay duchas con agua caliente?** *ay doochahs kohn ahgwah kahlyehnteh?*
– washing machines?	**¿Hay lavadoras?** *ay lahbahdohrahs?*
Is there a...on the site?	**¿En este camping hay...?** *ehn ehsteh kahmpeen ay...?*
Is there a children's play area on the site?	**¿En este camping hay un sitio para que jueguen los niños?** *ehn ehsteh kahmpeen ay oon seetyoh pahrah keh hwehghehn lohs neenyohs?*
Are there covered cooking facilities on the site?	**¿En este camping hay un sitio cubierto para cocinar?** *ehn ehsteh kahmpeen ay oon seetyoh koobyehrtoh pahrah kohtheenahr?*
Can I rent a safe here?	**¿Tienen caja fuerte para alquilar?** *tyehnehn kahhah fwehrteh pahrah ahlkeelahr?*
Are we allowed to barbecue here?	**¿Se pueden hacer barbacoas?** *seh pwehdehn ahthehr bahrbahkohahs?*
Are there any power points?	**¿Hay tomas de corriente eléctrica?** *ay tohmahs deh kohrryehnteh ehlehktreekah?*
Is there drinking water?	**¿Hay agua potable?** *ay ahgwah pohtahbleh?*
When's the rubbish collected?	**¿Cuándo pasan a recoger la basura?** *kwahndoh pahsahn ah rehkohhehr lah bahsoorah?*
Do you sell gas bottles (butane gas/propane gas)?	**¿Venden bombonas de gas (butano/propano)?** *behndehn bohmbohnahs deh gahs(bootahnoh/prohpahnoh)?*

7.3 Hotel/B&B/apartment/holiday house

Do you have a single/double room available?	**¿Le queda alguna habitación individual/doble?** *leh kehdah ahlgoonah ahbeetahthyohn eendeebeedwahl/dohbleh?*
per person/per room	**por persona/por habitación** *pohr pehrsohnah/pohr ahbeetahthyohn*
Does that include breakfast/lunch/ dinner?	**¿Incluye desayuno/comida/cena?** *eenklooyeh dehsahyoonoh/kohmeedah/thehnah?*
Could we have two adjoining rooms?	**¿Nos puede dar dos habitaciones una al lado de la otra?** *nohs pwehdeh dahr dohs ahbeetahthyohnehs oonah ahl lahdoh deh lah ohtrah?*
with/without toilet/bath/shower	**con/sin lavabo propio/baño propio/ducha propia** *kohn/seen lahbahboh prohpyoh/bahnyoh prohpyo/doochah prohpyah?*
(not) facing the street	**que (no) dé a la calle** *keh (noh) deh ah lah kahlyeh*
with/without a view of the sea	**con/sin vista al mar** *kohn/seen beestah ahl mahr*
Is there...in the hotel?	**¿El hotel tiene...?** *ehl ohtehl tyehneh...?*

Tiene lavabo y ducha en el mismo piso/en su habitación	You can find the toilet and shower on the same floor/en suite
Por aquí, por favor	This way, please
Su habitación está en el...piso; es la número...	Your room is on the...floor, number...

Is there a lift in the hotel?	¿El hotel tiene ascensor? *ehl ohtehl tyehneh ahsthehnsohr?*
Do you have room service?	¿El hotel tiene servicio de habitación? *ehl ohtehl tyehneh sehrbeethyoh deh ahbeetahthyohn?*
Could I see the room?	¿Puedo ver la habitación? *pwehdoh behr lah ahbeetahthyohn?*
I'll take this room	Me quedo con esta habitación *meh kehdoh kohn ehstah abeetathyohn*
We don't like this one	Esta no nos gusta *ehstah noh nohs goostah*
Do you have a larger/ less expensive room?	¿Tiene una habitación más grande/más barata? *tyehneh oonah ahbeetathyohn mahs grahnde/mahs bahrahtah?*
Could you put in a cot?	¿Puede agregar una cuna? *pwehde ahgrehgahr oonah koonah?*
What time's breakfast?	¿A qué hora es el desayuno? *ah keh ohrah ehs ehl dehsahyoonoh?*
Where's the dining room?	¿Dónde está el comedor? *dohndeh ehstah ehl kohmehdohr?*
Can I have breakfast in my room?	¿Me pueden traer el desayuno a la habitación? *meh pwehdehn trahehr ehl dehsahyoonoh ah lah ahbeetahthyohn?*
Where's the emergency exit/fire escape?	¿Dónde está la salida de emergencia/la escalera de incendios? *dohndeh ehstah lah sahleedah deh ehmehrhehnthyah/lah ehskahlehrah de eenthehndyohs?*
Where can I park my car (safely)?	¿Dónde hay un sitio (seguro) para aparcar el coche? *dohndeh ay oon seetyoh sehgooroh pahrah ahpahrkahr ehl kohcheh?*
The key to room..., please	La llave de la habitación..., por favor *lah lyahbeh deh lah ahbeetahthyohn..., pohr fahbohr*

Could you put this in the safe, please?	¿Podría dejar esto en la caja fuerte? *pohdreeah dehhahr ehstoh ehn lah cahhah fwehrteh?*
Could you wake me at...tomorrow?	¿Me podría despertar mañana a las...? *meh pohdreeah dehspehrtahr mahnyahnah ah lahs...?*
Could you find a babysitter for me?	¿Me podría conseguir una niñera para el bebé? *meh pohdreeah kohnsehgeer oonah neenyehrah pahrah ehl behbeh?*
Could I have an extra blanket?	¿Tendría una manta extra? *tehndreeah oonah mahntah ehxtrah?*
What days do the cleaners come in?	¿Qué días limpian la habitación? *keh deeahs leempyahn lah ahbeetahthyohn?*
When are the sheets/towels/tea towels changed?	¿Cuándo cambian las sábanas/las toallas/los paños de cocina? *kwahndoh kahmbyahn lahs sahbahnahs/lahs tohahlyahs/lohs pahnyohs deh kohtheenah?*

7.4 Complaints

We can't sleep for the noise	No podemos dormir por el ruido *noh pohdehmohs dohrmeer pohr ehl rweedoh*
Could you turn the radio down, please?	¿Podría bajar el volumen de la radio? *pohdreeah bahhahr ehl vohloomehn deh lah rahdyoh?*
We're out of toilet paper	Se ha acabado el papel higiénico. *seh ah ahkahbahdoh ehl pahpehl eehyehneekoh*
There aren't any.../there's not enough...	No hay.../no hay suficientes... *noh ay.../noh ay soofeethyehntehs...*

The bed linen's dirty ___	**La ropa de cama está sucia** *lah rohpah deh kahmah ehstah soothyah*
The room hasn't been cleaned.	**No han limpiado la habitación** *noh ahn leempyahdoh lah ahbeetahthyohn*
The kitchen is not clean	**La cocina no está limpia** *lah kohtheenah noh ehstah leempyah*
The kitchen utensils are dirty	**Los utensilios de cocina están sucios** *lohs ootehnseelyohs deh kohtheenah ehstahn soothyohs*
The heater's not working	**La calefacción no funciona** *lah kahlehfahkthyohn noh foonthyohnah*
There's no (hot) water/electricity	**No hay agua (caliente)/electricidad** *noh ay ahgwah(kahlyehnteh)/ehlehktreetheedahdh*
...is broken	**...está estropeado** *...ehstah ehstrohpehahdoh*
Could you have that seen to?	**¿Podrían hacerlo ver?** *pohdreeahn ahthehrloh behr?*
Could I have another room/site?	**¿Tendría otra habitación/sitio para la tienda?** *tehndreeah ohtrah abeetahthyohn/seetyoh pahrah lah tyehndah?*
The bed creaks terribly	**La cama hace mucho ruido** *lah kahmah ahtheh moochoh rweedoh*
The bed sags	**La cama es demasiado blanda** *lah kahmah ehs dehmahsyahdoh blahndah*
There are bugs/insects in our room	**Hay muchos bichos/insectos en nuestra habitación** *ay moochohs beechohs/eensehktohs ehn nwehstrah ahbeetahthyohn*
This place is full of mosquitos	**Está lleno de mosquitos** *ehstah lyehnoh deh mohskeetohs*
– cockroaches	**Está lleno de cucarachas** *ehstah lyehnoh deh kookahrahchahs*

7.5 Departure

See also 8.2 Settling the bill

I'm leaving tomorrow. Could I settle my bill, please?	**Mañana me voy. ¿Podría pagar la cuenta ahora?** *mahnyahnah meh boy. pohdreeah pahgahr lah kwehntah ahohrah?*
What time should we vacate?	**¿A qué hora tenemos que dejar...?** *ah keh ohrah tehnehmohs keh dehhahr...?*
Could I have my deposit/passport back, please?	**¿Me devuelve la fianza/el pasaporte?** *meh dehbwehlbeh lah fyahnthah/ehl pahsahpohrteh?*
We're in a terrible hurry	**Llevamos mucha prisa** *lyehbahmohs moochah preesah*
Could you forward my mail to this address?	**¿Podría enviarme la correspondencia a esta dirección?** *pohdreeah ehnbyahrmeh lah kohrrehspohndehnthyah ah ehstah deerehkthyohn?*
Could we leave our luggage here until we leave?	**¿Podríamos dejar las maletas aquí hasta que nos marchemos?** *pohdreeahmohs dehhahr lahs mahlehtahs ahkee ahstah keh nohs mahrchehmohs?*
Thanks for your hospitality	**Muchas gracias por la hospitalidad** *moochahs grahthyahs pohr lah ohspeetahleedahdh*

8 Money matters

● **In general**, banks are open between 9am and 2pm; they are closed on Saturdays. In large cities some main branches open until 4.30. To exchange currency a passport is required. The sign *cambio* indicates that money can be exchanged.

8.1 Banks

Where can I find a bank/an exchange office around here? ____ ¿Dónde hay un banco/una oficina de cambios por aquí?
dohndeh ay oon bahnkoh/oonah ohfeetheenah deh kahmbyohs pohr ahkee?

Where can I cash this traveller's cheque/giro cheque? ____ ¿Dónde puedo cambiar este cheque de viajero/este cheque postal?
dohndeh pwehdoh kahmbyahr ehsteh chehkeh deh byahhehroh/ehsteh chehkeh pohstahl?

Can I cash this...here? ____ ¿Puedo cambiar aquí este...?
pwehdoh kahmbyahr ahkee ehsteh...?

Can I withdraw money on my credit card here? ____ ¿Se puede sacar dinero con una tarjeta de crédito?
seh pwehdeh sahkahr deenehroh kohn oonah tahrhehtah deh krehdeetoh?

What's the minimum/maximum amount? ____ ¿Cuál es el mínimo/el máximo?
kwahl ehs ehl meeneemoh/ehl mahxeemoh?

Can I take out less than that? ____ ¿También puedo sacar menos?
tahmbyehn pwehdoh sahkahr mehnohs?

I've had some money transferred here. Has it arrived yet? ____ He pedido un giro telegráfico. ¿Me ha llegado ya?
eh pehdeedoh oon heeroh tehlehgrahfeekoh. meh ah lyehgahdoh yah?

These are the details of my bank in the UK ____ Estos son los datos de mi banco en el Reino Unido
ehstohs sohn lohs dahtohs deh mee bahnkoh ehn ehl reynoh ooneedoh

Firme aquí	Sign here, please
Tiene que rellenar esto	Fill this out, please
¿Me permite su pasaporte?	Could I see your passport, please?
¿Me permite su carnet de identidad?	Could I see some identification, please?
¿Me permite su tarjeta de la caja postal?	Could I see your girobank card, please?
¿Me permite su tarjeta del banco?	Could I see your bank card, please?

This is my bank/giro number ___ **Este es mi número de cuenta bancaria/de la caja postal** *ehsteh ehs mee noomehroh deh kwehntah bahnkahryah/deh lah kahhah pohstahl*

I'd like to change some money ___ **Quisiera cambiar dinero** *keesyehrah kahmbyahr deenehroh*

– pounds into... ___ **Libras esterlinas por...** *leebrahs ehstehrleenahs pohr...*

– dollars into... ___ **Dólares estadounidenses por...** *dohlahrehs ehstahdohooneedehnsehs pohr...*

What's the exchange rate? ___ **¿A cuánto está el cambio?** *ah kwahntoh ehstah ehl kahmbyoh?*

Could you give me some small change with it? ___ **¿Me podría dar sencillo/cambio?** *meh pohdreeah dahr sehntheelyoh/kahmbyoh?*

This is not right ___ **Esto está mal** *ehstoh ehstah mahl*

No aceptamos tarjetas de crédito/cheques de viajero/moneda extranjera	We don't accept credit cards/traveller's cheques/foreign currency

8.2 Settling the bill

Could you put it on my bill?	**¿Podría cargarlo a mi cuenta?** *pohdreeah kahrgahrloh ah mee kwehntah?*
Does this amount include service?	**¿Está incluido el servicio en esta cifra?** *ehstah eenklooeedoh ehl sehrbeethyoh ehn ehstah theefrah?*
Can I pay by...?	**¿Puedo pagar con...?** *pwehdoh pahgahr kohn...?*
Can I pay by credit card?	**¿Puedo pagar con tarjeta de crédito?** *pwehdoh pahgahr kohn tahrhehtah deh krehdeetoh?*
Can I pay by traveller's cheque?	**¿Puedo pagar con un cheque de viajero?** *pwehdoh pahgahr kohn oon chehkeh de byahhehroh?*
Can I pay with foreign currency?	**¿Puedo pagar con moneda extranjera?** *pwehdoh pahgahr kohn mohnehdah ehxtrahnhehrah?*
You've given me too much/you haven't given me enough change	**Me ha devuelto de más/de menos** *meh ah dehbwehltoh deh mahs/deh mehnohs*
Could you check the bill again, please?	**¿Puede volver a hacer la cuenta?** *pwehdeh bohlbehr ah ahthehr lah kwehntah?*
Could I have a receipt, please?	**¿Podría darme un recibo?** *pohdreeah dahrmeh oon rehtheeboh?*
I don't have enough money on me	**No me alcanza el dinero** *noh meh ahlkahnthah ehl deenehroh*
This is for you	**Tenga, esto es para usted** *tehngah, ehstoh ehs pahrah oostehdh*
Keep the change	**Quédese con la vuelta** *kehdehseh kohn lah bwehlta*

9 Post and telephone

9.1 Post

For giros, see 8 Money matters

● **Post offices** are open from Monday to Saturday from 9am to 1 or 1.30pm. However stamps (*sellos*) can be bought at any *estanco* and many hotels also provide stamps. It is advisable to post letters at a post office, rather than the yellow mail boxes (*buzón*).

giros postales	telegramas	sellos
money orders	telegrams	stamps
paquetes		
parcels		

Where's...? ¿Dónde está...?
dohndeh ehstah...?

Where's the post office? ¿Dónde hay una oficina de Correos por aquí?
dohndeh ay oonah ohfeetheenah deh kohrrehohs pohr ahkee?

Where's the main post office? ¿Dónde está la oficina central de Correos?
dohndeh ehstah lah ohfeetheenah thehntrahl deh kohrrehohs?

Where's the postbox? ¿Dónde hay un buzón por aquí?
dohndeh ahee oon boothohn pohr ahkee?

Which counter should I go to...? ¿Cuál es la ventanilla para...?
kwahl ehs lah behntahneelyah pahrah...?

– to send a fax ¿Cuál es la ventanilla para enviar un fax?
kwahl ehs lah behntahneelyah pahrah ehnbyahr oon fahx?

– to change money	**¿Cuál es la ventanilla para cambiar dinero?** *kwahl ehs lah behntahneelyah pahrah kahmbyahr deenehroh?*
– to change giro cheques	**¿Cuál es la ventanilla para los cheques postales?** *kwahl ehs lah behntahneelyah pahrah lohs chehkehs pohstahlehs?*
– for a Telegraph Money Order?	**¿Cuál es la ventanilla para los giros telegráficos?** *kwahl ehs lah behntahneelyah pahrah lohs heerohs tehlehgrahfeekohs?*
Poste restante	**Lista de correos** *leestah deh kohrrehohs*
Is there any mail for me? My name's...	**¿Hay carta para mí? Me llamo...** *ay kahrtah pahrah mee? meh lyahmoh...*

Stamps

What's the postage for a...to...?	**¿Cuánto se le pone a un(a)...para...?** *kwahntoh seh leh pohneh ah oon(ah)...pahrah...?*
Are there enough stamps on it?	**¿Lleva suficiente franqueo?** *lyehbah soofeethyehnteh frahnkehoh?*
I'd like... ...euro stamps	**Déme...sellos de...** *dehmeh...sehlyohs deh...*
I'd like to send this...	**Quisiera enviar esto...** *keesyehrah ehnbyahr ehstoh...*
– express	**Quisiera enviar esto por correo urgente** *keesyehrah ehnbyahr ehstoh pohr kohrrehoh oorhehnteh*
– by air mail	**Quisiera enviar esto por avión** *keesyehrah ehnbyahr ehstoh pohr ahbyohn*
– by registered mail	**Quisiera enviar esto certificado** *keesyehrah ehnbyahr ehstoh thehrteefeekahdoh*

Telegram/fax

I'd like to send a telegram to...	**Quisiera mandar un telegrama a...** *keesyehrah mahndahr oon tehlehgrahmah ah...*
How much is that per word?	**¿Cuánto cuesta por palabra?** *kwahntoh kwehstah pohr pahlahbrah?*
This is the text I want to send	**Este es el texto que quiero enviar** *ehsteh ehs ehl tehxtoh keh kyehroh ehnbyahr*
Shall I fill in the form myself?	**¿Relleno yo mismo el formulario?** *rehlyehnoh yoh meesmoh ehl fohrmoolahryoh?*
Can I make photocopies/ send a fax here?	**¿Se pueden hacer fotocopias/se puede enviar un fax aquí?** *seh pwehdehn ahthehr fohtohkohpyahs/seh pwehdeh ehnbyahr oon fahx ahkee?*
How much is it per page?	**¿Cuánto cuesta por página?** *kwahntoh kwehstah pohr pahheenah?*

9.2 Telephone

See also 1.8 Telephone alphabet

● **All phone booths** offer a direct international service to the UK or US (07 - country code 44 (UK) or 1 (US) – trunk code minus 0 – number). Area codes are displayed. It is easier, and may even be cheaper to place your call from the *Telefónica* or telephone office. When phoning someone in Spain, you will not be greeted with the subscriber's name but diga or *dígame*.

Is there a phone box around here?	**¿Hay alguna cabina teléfonica por aquí?** *ay ahlgoonah kahbeenah tehlehfohneekah pohr ahkee?*

Could I use your phone, please?	¿Podría usar su teléfono? *pohdreeah oosahr soo tehlehfohnoh?*
Do you have a (city/region)...phone directory?	¿Tiene una guía de teléfonos de la ciudad/la provincia de...? *tyehneh oonah gheeah deh tehlehfohnohs deh lah thyoodahdh/lah prohbeenthyah deh...?*
Where can I get a phone card?	¿Dónde puedo conseguir una tarjeta de teléfonos? *dohndeh pwehdoh kohnsehgheer oonah tahrhehtah deh tehlehfohnohs?*
Could you give me...?	¿Me podría dar...? *meh pohdreeah dahr...?*
– the number for international directory enquiries	¿Me podría dar el número de información internacional? *meh pohdreeah dahr ehl noomehroh deh eenfohrmahthyohn eentehrnahthyohnahl?*
– the number of room...	¿Me podría dar el número de la habitación...? *meh pohdreeah dahr ehl noomehroh deh lah ahbeetahthyohn...?*
– the international access code	¿Me podría dar el indicativo internacional? *meh pohdreeah dahr ehl eendeekahteeboh eentehrnahthyonahl...?*
– the country code for...	¿Me podría dar el indicativo de...? *meh pohdreeah dahr ehl eendeekahteeboh deh...?*
– the trunk code for...	¿Me podría dar el prefijo de...? *meh pohdreeah dahr ehl prehfeehoh deh...?*
– the number of...	¿Me podría dar el número de abonado de...? *meh pohdreeah dahr ehl noomehroh deh ahbohnahdoh deh...?*

Could you check if this number's correct?	**¿Podría controlar si está bien este número?** *pohdreeah kohntrohlahr see ehstah byehn ehsteh noomehroh?*
Can I dial international direct?	**¿Se puede llamar directamente al extranjero?** *seh pwehdeh lyahmahr deerehktahmehnteh ahl ehxtrahnhehroh?*
Do I have to go through the switchboard?	**¿Hay que llamar por operadora?** *ay keh lyahmahr pohr ohpehrahdohrah?*
Do I have to dial '0' first?	**¿Hay que marcar primero el cero?** *ay keh mahrkahr preemehroh ehl thehroh?*
Do I have to book my calls?	**¿Hay que pedir línea?** *ay keh pehdeer leenehah?*
Could you dial this number for me, please?	**¿Podría usted llamar a este número?** *pohdreeah oostehdh lyahmahr ah ehsteh noomehroh?*
Could you put me through to.../extension..., please?	**¿Me podría poner con.../con la extensión...?** *meh pohdreeah pohnehr kohn.../kohn lah ehxtehnsyohn...?*
I'd like to place a reverse-charge call to...	**Quisiera una llamada de cobro revertido a...** *keesyehrah oonah lyahmahdah deh kohbroh rehbehrteedoh ah...*
What's the charge per minute?	**¿Cuánto cuesta por minuto?** *kwahntoh kwehstah pohr meenootoh?*
Have there been any calls for me?	**¿Ha habido alguna llamada para mí?** *ah ahbeedoh ahlgoonah lyahmahdah pahrah mee?*

The conversation

Hello, this is...	Buenos días, soy... *bwehnohs deeahs, soy...*
Who is this, please?	¿Con quién hablo? *kohn kyehn ahbloh?*
Is this...?	¿Hablo con...? *ahbloh kohn...?*
I'm sorry, I've dialled the wrong number	Perdone, me he equivocado de número *pehrdohneh, meh eh ehkeebohkahdoh deh noomehroh*
I can't hear you	No le oigo bien *noh leh oygoh byehn*
I'd like to speak to...	Quisiera hablar con... *keesyehrah ahblahr kohn...*
Is there anybody who speaks English?	¿Hay alguien que hable inglés? *ay ahlghyehn keh ahbleh eenglehs?*

Lo llaman por teléfono	There's a phone call for you
Primero tiene que marcar el cero	You have to dial '0' first
Un momento, por favor	One moment, please
No contestan	There's no answer
Está comunicando	The line's engaged
¿Quiere esperar?	Do you want to hold?
Ahora le paso	Putting you through
Se ha equivocado de número	You've got a wrong number
El señor/la señora...no está en estos momentos.	He's/she's not here right now
El señor/la señora...no estará hasta...	He'll/she'll be back...
Este es el contestador automático de...	This is the answering machine of...

Extension..., please	¿Me pone con la extensión...? *meh pohneh kohn lah ehxtehnsyohn...?*
Could you ask him/her to call me back?	¿Podría decirle que me llame? *pohdreeah dehtheerleh keh meh lyahmeh?*
My name's... My number's...	Me llamo...Mi número es... *meh lyahmoh...mee noomehroh ehs...*
Could you tell him/her I called?	¿Puede decirle que he llamado? *pwehdeh dehtheerleh keh eh lyahmahdoh?*
I'll call back tomorrow	Lo/la volveré a llamar mañana *loh/lah bohlbehreh ah lyahmahr mahnyahnah*

10 Shopping

● **Opening times:** Mon–Fri, 9.30–1.30 and 5–8. Department stores are open in the afternoons from 4pm and remain open on Saturdays. Other shops generally close on Saturdays at 1pm. In tourist areas shops open for longer periods. Chemists display the list of *farmacias de guardia* (those open on Sundays and after hours).

10.1 Shopping conversations

Where can I get...?	**¿Dónde puedo conseguir...?** *dohndeh pwehdoh kohnsehgheer...?*
When does this shop open?	**¿De qué hora a qué hora abren?** *deh keh ohrah ah keh ohrah ahbrehn?*
Could you tell me where the...department is?	**¿Me podría indicar la sección de...?** *meh pohdreeah eendeekahr lah sehkthyohn deh...?*
Could you help me, please? I'm looking for...	**¿Podría ayudarme? Busco...** *pohdreeah ahyoodahrmeh? booskoh...*
Do you sell British/American newspapers?	**¿Venden periódicos británicos/americanos?** *behndehn pehryohdeekohs breetahneekohs/ahmehreekahnohs?*

¿Lo/la atienden? — Are you being served?

No, I'd like...	**No. Quisiera...** *noh. keesyehrah...*
I'm just looking, if that's all right	**Sólo estoy mirando, gracias** *sohloh ehstoy meerahndoh, grahthyahs*

¿Algo más? — Anything else?

almacén
department store
antigüedades
antiques
artículos de deporte
sports shop
artículos del hogar
household goods
artículos dietéticos
health food shop
artículos fotográficos
camera shop
artículos usados
second hand goods
autoservicio
self service
bicicletas
bicycle shop
bodega
off licence
bricolaje
DIY-store
carnicería
butcher's shop
casa de música
music shop
centro comercial
shopping centre
comestibles
grocery store
decoración (de interiores)
interior design shop
droguería
household products and cosmetics
electrodomésticos
electrical appliances
estanco
tobacconist
farmacia
chemist
ferretería
hardware shop
floristería
florist
frutas y verduras
greengrocer
galería comercial
shopping arcade
heladería
ice cream parlour
joyería
jeweller
juguetería
toy shop
lavandería
laundry
lechería
dairy
librería
book shop
mercado
market
mercería
draper
óptica
optician
panadería
bakery
pastelería
cake shop
peluquería (señoras, caballeros)
hairdresser
perfumería
cosmetics
pescadería
fishmonger
quiosco
news stand
recuerdos de viaje
souvenir shop
reparación de bicicletas
bicycle repair shop
revistas y prensa
newsagent
salón de belleza
beauty parlour
supermercado
supermarket
tienda
shop
tienda de modas
clothes shop
tintorería
drycleaner
zapatería
shoe shop
zapatero
cobbler

Yes, I'd also like...	Sí, también déme... *see, tahmbyehn dehmeh...*
No, thank you. That's all	No, gracias. Es todo *noh, grahthyahs, ehs tohdoh*
Could you show me...?	¿Me podría mostrar...? *meh pohdreeah mohstrahr...?*
I'd prefer...	Prefiero... *prehfyehroh...*
This is not what I'm looking for	No es lo que busco *noh ehs loh keh booskoh*
Thank you. I'll keep looking	Gracias. Voy a seguir mirando *grahthyahs. boy ah sehgheer meerahndoh*
Do you have something...?	¿No tendría algo ...? *noh tehndreeah ahlgoh ...?*
– less expensive?	¿No tendría algo más barato? *noh tehndreeah ahlgoh mahs bahrahtoh?*
– smaller?	¿No tendría algo más pequeño? *noh tehndreeah ahlgoh mahs pehkehnyoh?*
– larger?	¿No tendría algo más grande? *noh tehndreeah ahlgoh mahs grahndeh?*
I'll take this one	Me llevo éste/ésta *meh lyehboh ehsteh/ehstah*

Lo siento; no lo tenemos	I'm sorry, we don't have that
Lo siento; ya no queda	I'm sorry, we're sold out
Lo siento, hasta el...no lo tendremos	I'm sorry, that won't be in until...
Pague en la caja, por favor	You can pay at the cash desk
No aceptamos tarjetas de crédito	We don't accept credit cards
No aceptamos cheques de viajero	We don't accept traveller's cheques
No aceptamos moneda extranjera	We don't accept foreign currency

Does it come with instructions?	**¿Viene con instrucciones?** *byehneh kohn eenstrookthyohnehs?*
It's too expensive	**Me parece muy caro** *meh pahrehtheh mwee kahroh*
I'll give you...	**Le doy...** *leh doy...*
Could you keep this for me? I'll come back for it later	**¿Me lo/la podría guardar? Volveré más tarde a buscarlo** *meh loh/lah pohdreeah gwahrdahr? bohlbehreh mahs tahrdeh ah booskahrloh*
Have you got a bag for me, please?	**¿Tendría una bolsita?** *tehndreeah oonah bohlseetah?*
Could you giftwrap it, please?	**¿Me lo podría envolver para regalo?** *meh loh pohdreeah ehnbohlbehr pahrah rehgahloh?*

10.2 Food

I'd like a hundred grams of..., please	**Quisiera cien gramos de...** *keesyehrah thyehn grahmohs deh...*
– half a kilo of...	**Quisiera medio kilo de...** *keesyehrah mehdyoh keeloh deh...*
– a kilo of...	**Quisiera un kilo de...** *keesyehrah oon keeloh deh...*
Could you...it for me, please?	**¿Me lo podría...?** *meh loh pohdreeah...?*
Could you slice it/dice it for me, please?	**¿Me lo podría cortar en lonchas/en trozos?** *meh loh pohdreeah kohrtahr ehn lohnchahs/ehn trohthohs?*
Could you grate it for me, please?	**¿Me lo podría rallar?** *meh loh pohdreeah rahlyahr?*
Can I order it?	**¿Se lo podría encargar?** *seh loh pohdreeah ehnkahrgahr?*
I'll pick it up tomorrow/at...	**Pasaré a buscarlo mañana/a las...** *pahsahreh ah booskahrloh mahnyahnah/ah lahs...*

Can you eat/drink this?	**¿Es para comer/beber?** *ehs pahrah kohmehr/behbehr?*
What's in it?	**¿Qué lleva dentro?** *keh lyehbah dehntroh?*

10.3 Clothing and shoes

I saw something in the window. Shall I point it out?	**He visto algo en el escaparate. ¿Se lo enseño?** *eh beestoh ahlgoh ehn ehl ehskahpahrahteh, seh loh ehnsehnyoh?*
I'd like something to go with this	**Busco algo que haga juego con esto** *booskoh ahlgoh keh ahgah hwehgoh kohn ehstoh*
Do you have shoes in this colour?	**¿Tiene zapatos de este color?** *tyehneh thahpahtohs deh ehsteh kohlohr?*
I'm a size...in the UK	**En el Reino Unido tengo el número...** *ehn ehl reheenoh ooneedoh tehngoh ehl noomehroh...*
Can I try this on?	**¿Me lo podría probar?** *meh loh pohdreeah prohbahr?*
Where's the fitting room?	**¿Dónde está el probador?** *dohndeh ehstah ehl prohbahdohr?*
It doesn't fit	**No me vale** *noh meh bahleh*
This is the right size	**Este es mi número** *ehsteh ehs mee noomehroh*
It doesn't suit me	**No me está bien** *noh meh ehstah byehn*
Do you have this/these in...?	**¿Tiene éste/ésta, pero en...?** *tyehneh ehsteh/ehstah pehroh ehn...?*
The heel's too high/low	**El tacón me parece muy alto/bajo** *ehl tahkohn meh pahrehtheh mwee ahltoh/bahhoh*
Is this/are these genuine leather?	**¿Es/son de piel auténtica?** *ehs/sohn deh pyehl ah-ootehnteekah?*

No planchar	Colgar mojado	Lavado a mano
Do not iron	Drip dry	Hand wash
No centrifugar	Lavado en seco	Lavado a máquina
Do not spin dry	Dry clean	Machine wash

I'm looking for a... for a...-year-old baby/child	Busco un/una...para un bebé/niño de...años *booskoh oon/oonah...pahrah oon behbeh/neenyoh deh...ahnyohs*
I'd like a... ...	Quisiera un/una...de... *keesyehrah oon/oonah...deh...*
– silk	Quisiera un/una...de seda *keesyehrah oon/oonah...deh sehdah*
– cotton	Quisiera un/una...de algodón *keesyehrah oon/oonah...deh ahlgohdohn*
– woollen	Quisiera un/una...de lana *keesyehrah oon/oonah...deh lahnah*
– linen	Quisiera un/una...de hilo *keesyehrah oon/oonah...deh eeloh*
What temperature can I wash it at?	¿A qué temperatura lo puedo lavar? *ah keh tehmpehrahtoorah loh pwehdoh lahbahr?*
Will it shrink in the wash?	¿Encoge al lavarlo? *enkohheh ahl lahbahrloh?*

At the cobbler

Could you mend these shoes?	¿Podría arreglar estos zapatos? *pohdreeah ahrrehglahr ehstohs thahpahtohs?*
Could you put new soles/heels on these?	¿Podría ponerle nuevas suelas/nuevos tacones? *pohdreeah pohnehrleh nwehbahs swehlahs/nwehbohs tahkohnehs?*
When will they be ready?	¿Para cuándo van a estar? *pahrah kwahndoh bahn ah ehstahr?*

I'd like..., please ______ Quisiera..., por favor
keesyehrah..., pohr fahbohr

– a tin of shoe polish___ Quisiera una crema para zapatos
keesyehrah oonah krehmah pahrah thahpahtohs

– a pair of shoelaces___ Quisiera un par de cordones
keesyehrah oon pahr deh kohrdohnehs

10.4 Photographs and video

I'd like a film for this camera, please ___ Quisiera un rollo/carrete para esta cámara
keesyehrah oon rohlyoh/kahrrehteh pahrah ehstah kahmahrah

– a 126 cartridge _____ Quisiera una película en cassette de 126
keesyehrah oonah pehleekoolah ehn kahseht deh thyehntoh beheenteesehees

– a 35mm colour slide__ Un carrete de 35mm para diapositivas en color
oon kahrrehteh deh treyntah ee theenkoh meeleemehtrohs pahrah deeapohseeteebahs ehn kohlohr

– a 35mm colour print _____ Un carrete de 35mm en color
oon kahrrehteh deh treyntah ee theenkoh meeleemehtrohs ehn kohlohr

– a 35mm black and white ______ Un carrete de 35mm en blanco y negro
oon kahrrehteh deh treyntah ee theenkoh meeleemehtrohs ehn blahnkoh ee nehgroh

– a videotape _______ Quisiera una cinta de vídeo
keesyehrah oonah theentah deh veedehoh

colour/black and white _ color/blanco y negro
kohlohr/blahnkoh ee nehgroh

super eight _________ superocho
soopehrohchoh

12/24/36 exposures	doce/veinticuatro/treinta y seis fotos *dohtheh/beheenteekwahtroh/treheentah ee sehees fohtohs*
ASA/DIN number	valor ISO *bahlohr eesoh*
daylight film	película para luz natural *pehleekoolah pahrah looth nahtoorahl*
film for artificial light	película para luz artificial *pehleekoolah pahrah looth ahrteefeethyah*

Problems

Could you load the film for me, please?	¿Me podría poner el rollo/carrete en la cámara? *meh pohdreeah pohnehr ehl rohlyoh/kahrrehteh ehn lah kahmahrah?*
Could you take the film out for me, please?	¿Me podría sacar el rollo/carrete de la cámara? *meh pohdreeah sahkahr ehl rohlyoh/kahrrehteh deh lah kahmahrah?*
Should I replace the batteries?	¿Tengo que cambiar las pilas? *tehngoh keh kahmbyahr lahs peelahs?*
Could you have a look at my camera, please? It's not working	¿Me podría revisar la cámara? Ya no funciona *meh pohdreeah rehbeesahr lah kahmahrah? yah noh foonthyohnah*
The...is broken	Está estropeado el... *ehstah ehstrohpehahdoh ehl...*
The film's jammed	Se ha atascado el rollo/carrete *seh ah ahtahskahdoh ehl rohlyoh/kahrrehteh*
The film's broken	Se ha roto el rollo/carrete *seh ah rohtoh ehl rohlyoh/kahrrehteh*
The flash isn't working	No funciona el flash *noh foonthyohnah ehl flahsh*

Processing and prints

I'd like to have this film developed/printed, please	**Quisiera mandar a revelar/copiar este rollo/carrete** *keesyehrah mahndahr ah rehbehlahr/kohpyahr ehsteh rohlyoh/kahrrehteh*
I'd like...prints from each negative	**Quisiera...copias de cada negativo** *keesyehrah...kohpyahs deh kahdah nehgahteeboh*
glossy/mat	**brillante/mate** *breelyahnte/mahteh*
I'd like to reorder these photos	**Quisiera encargar más copias de estas fotos** *keesyehrah ehnkahrgahr mahs kohpyahs deh ehstahs fohtohs*
I'd like to have this photo enlarged	**Quisiera una ampliación de esta foto** *keesyehrah oonah ahmplyahthyohn deh ehstah fohtoh*
How much is processing?	**¿Cuánto sale el revelado?** *kwahntoh sahleh ehl rehbehlahdoh?*
– printing?	**¿Cuánto sale el copiado?** *kwahntoh sahleh ehl kohpyahdoh?*
– extra copies?	**¿Cuánto salen las copias adicionales?** *kwahntoh sahlehn lahs kohpyahs ahdeethyohnahlehs?*
– the enlargement?	**¿Cuánto sale la ampliación?** *kwahntoh sahleh lah ahmplyahthyohn?*
When will they be ready?	**¿Para cuándo van a estar?** *pahrah kwahndoh bahn ah ehstahr?*

10.5 At the hairdresser's

Do I have to make an appointment?	**¿Tengo que pedir hora?** *tehngoh keh pehdeer ohrah?*

Can I come in straight away?	¿Podría atenderme en seguida? *pohdreeah ahtehndehrmeh ehn sehgheedah?*
How long will I have to wait?	¿Cuánto tengo que esperar? *kwahntoh tehngoh keh ehspehrahr?*
I'd like a shampoo/ haircut	Quisiera lavarme/cortarme el pelo *keesyehrah lahbahrmeh/kohrtahrmeh ehl pehloh*
I'd like a shampoo for oily/dry hair, please	Quisiera un champú para cabello graso/seco *keesyehrah oon chahmpoo pahrah kahbehlyoh grahsoh/sehkoh*
an anti-dandruff shampoo	Quisiera un champú anticaspa *keesyehrah oon chahmpoo ahnteekahspah*
– a shampoo for permed/coloured hair	Quisiera un champú para cabello con permanente/teñido. *keesyehrah oon chahmpoo pahrah kahbehlyoh kohn pehrmahnehnteh/tehnyeedoh*
– a colour rinse shampoo	Quisiera un champú color *keesyehrah oon chahmpoo kohlohr*
– a shampoo with conditioner	Quisiera un champú con acondicionador *keesyehrah oon chahmpoo kohn ahkohndeethyohnahdohr*
– highlights	Quisiera que me hagan claritos *keesyehrah keh meh ahgahn klahreetohs*
Do you have a colour chart, please?	¿Tendría una carta de colores? *tehndreeah oonah kahrtah deh kohlohrehs?*
I want to keep it the same colour	Quiero conservar el mismo color *kyehroh kohnsehrbahr ehl meesmoh kohlohr*
I'd like it darker/lighter	Quisiera un color más oscuro/más claro *keesyehrah oon kohlohr mahs ohskooroh/mahs klahroh*
I'd like/I don't want hairspray	(No) quiero fijador *(noh) kyehroh feehahdohr*

– gel	(No) quiero gel *(noh) kyehroh hehl*
– lotion	(No) quiero loción *(noh) kyehroh lohthyohn*
I'd like a short fringe	Quisiera el flequillo corto *keesyehrah ehl flehkeelyoh kohrtoh*
Not too short at the back	No lo quisiera demasiado corto por detrás *noh loh keesyehrah dehmahsyahdoh kohrtoh pohr dehtrahs*
Not too long here	No lo quisiera demasiado largo aquí *noh loh keesyehrah dehmahsyahdoh lahrgoh ahkee*
I'd like/I don't want (many) curls	(No) quisiera (demasiados) rizos *(noh) keesyehrah (dehmahsyadohs) reethohs*
It needs a little/a lot taken off	Hay que cortar sólo un trocito/un buen trozo *ay keh kohrtahr sohloh oon trohtheetoh/oon bwehn trohthoh*
I want a completely different style	Quisiera un modelo totalmente diferente *keesyehrah oon mohdehloh tohtahlmehnteh deefehrehnteh*
I'd like it the same as...	Quisiera el pelo como... *keesyehrah ehl pehloh kohmoh...*
– as that lady's	Quisiera el pelo como esa señora *keesyehrah ehl pehloh kohmoh ehsah sehnyohrah*
– as in this photo	Quisiera el pelo como en esta foto *keesyehrah ehl pehloh kohmoh ehn ehstah fohtoh*
Could you put the drier up/down a bit?	¿Podría poner el casco más alto/bajo? *pohdreeah pohnehr ehl kahskoh mahs ahltoh/ bahhoh?*
I'd like a facial	Quisiera una máscara facial *keesyehrah oonah mahskahrah fahthyahl*

– a manicure	**Quisiera que me hagan manicura** *keesyehrah keh meh ahgahn mahneekoorah*
– a massage	**Quisiera que me hagan masaje** *keesyehrah keh meh ahgahn mahsahheh*
Could you trim my fringe?	**¿Me podría recortar el flequillo?** *meh pohdreeah rehkohrtahr ehl flehkeelyoh?*
– my beard?	**¿Me podría recortar la barba?** *meh pohdreeah rehkohrtahr lah bahrbah?*
– my moustache?	**¿Me podría recortar el bigote?** *meh pohdreeah rehkohrtahr ehl beegohteh?*
I'd like a shave, please	**Aféiteme, por favor** *ahfeheetehmeh, pohr fahbohr*
I'd like a wet shave, please	**Aféiteme a navaja, por favor** *ahfeheetehmeh ah nahbahhah, pohr fahbohr*

¿Cómo quiere el corte de pelo?	How do you want it cut?
¿Qué modelo deseaba?	What style did you have in mind?
¿Qué color quiere?	What colour do you want it?
¿Esta temperatura le va bien?	Is the temperature all right for you?
¿Quiere algo para leer?	Would you like something to read?
¿Quiere algo para beber?	Would you like a drink?
¿Así está bien?	Is this what you had in mind?

11 At the Tourist Information Centre

11.1 Places of interest

Where's the Tourist Information, please?	¿Dónde está la oficina de turismo? *dohndeh ehstah lah ohfeetheenah deh tooreesmoh?*
Do you have a city map?	¿Tendría un plano de la ciudad? *tehndreeah oon plahnoh deh lah thyoodahdh?*
Where is the museum?	¿Dónde está el museo? *dohndeh ehstah ehl moosehoh?*
Where can I find a church?	¿Dónde podría encontrar una iglesia? *dohndeh pohdreeah ehnkohntrahr oonah eeglehsyah?*
Could you give me some information about...?	¿Me podría dar información sobre...? *meh pohdreeah dahr eenfohrmahthyohn sohbreh...?*
How much is that?	¿Cuánto le debemos por esto? *kwahntoh leh dehbehmohs pohr ehstoh?*
What are the main places of interest?	¿Cuáles son los sitios más interesantes para visitar? *kwahlehs sohn lohs seetyohs mahs eentehrehsahntehs pahrah veeseetahr?*
Could you point them out on the map?	¿Me los podría señalar en el plano? *meh lohs pohdreeah sehnyahlahr ehn ehl plahnoh?*
What do you recommend?	¿Qué nos recomienda? *keh nohs rehkohmyehndah?*
We'll be here for a few hours	Pensamos quedarnos unas horas *pehnsahmohs kehdahrnohs oonahs ohrahs*
– a day	Pensamos quedarnos un día *pehnsahmohs kehdahrnohs oon deeah*
– a week	Pensamos quedarnos una semana *pehnsahmohs kehdahrnohs oonah sehmahnah*
We're interested in...	Nos interesa... *nohs eentehrehsah...*

Is there a scenic walk around the city?	**¿Hay algún circuito turístico para visitar la ciudad a pie?** *ay ahlgoon theerkweetoh tooreesteekoh pahrah veeseetar lah thyoodahdh ah pyeh?*
How long does it take?	**¿Cuánto dura?** *kwahntoh doorah?*
Where does it start/end?	**¿De dónde sale?/¿Dónde termina?** *deh dohndeh sahleh?/dohndeh tehrmeenah?*
Are there any boat cruises here?	**¿Hay excursiones en barco?** *ay ehxkoorsyohnehs ehn bahrkoh?*
Where can we board?	**¿Dónde se puede embarcar?** *dohndeh seh pwehdeh ehmbahrkahr?*
Are there any bus tours?	**¿Hay excursiones en autocar?** *ay ehxkoorsyohnehs ehn ahootohkahr?*
Where do we get on?	**¿De dónde salen?** *deh dohndeh sahlehn?*
Is there a guide who speaks English?	**¿Hay algún guía que hable inglés?** *ay ahlgoon gheeah keh ahbleh eenglehs?*
What trips can we take around the area?	**¿Qué excursiones se pueden hacer en los alrededores?** *keh ehxkoorsyohnehs seh pwehdehn ahthehr ehn lohs ahlrehdehdohrehs?*
Are there any excursions?	**¿Hay excursiones organizadas?** *ay ehxkoorsyohnehs ohrgahneethahdahs?*
Where do they go to?	**¿Hacia dónde van?** *ahthyah dohndeh bahn?*
We'd like to go to...	**Quisiéramos ir a...** *keesyehrahmohs eer ah...*
How long is the trip?	**¿Cuánto se tarda en llegar?** *kwahntoh seh tahrdah ehn lyehgahr?*
How long do we stay in...?	**¿Cuánto dura la visita a...?** *kwahntoh doorah lah beeseetah ah...*
Are there any guided tours?	**¿Hay visitas guiadas?** *ay beeseetahs gheeahdahs?*

How much free time will we have there?	¿Cuánto tiempo libre tenemos allí? *kwahntoh tyehmpoh leebreh tehnehmohs alyee?*
We want to go hiking	Nos gustaría hacer una excursión a pie *nohs goostahreeah ahthehr oonah ehxkoorsyohn ah pyeh*
Can we hire a guide?	¿Es posible contratar un guía? *ehs pohseebleh kohntrahtahr oon gheeah?*
Can I book mountain huts?	¿Se puede hacer una reserva para un refugio (en la montaña)? *seh pwehdeh ahthehr oonah rehsehrbah pahrah oon rehfoohyoh (ehn lah mohntahnyah)?*
What time does... open/close?	¿A qué hora abre/cierra...? *ah keh ohrah ahbreh/thyehrrah...?*
What days is...open/ closed?	¿Qué días tiene abierto/cerrado...? *keh deeahs tyehneh ahbyehrtoh/thehrrahdoh...?*
What's the admission price?	¿Cuánto sale la entrada? *kwahntoh sahleh lah ehntrahdah?*
Is there a group discount?	¿Hay descuento para grupos? *ay dehskwehntoh pahrah groopohs?*
Is there a child discount?	¿Hay descuento para niños? *ay dehskwehntoh pahrah neenyohs?*
Is there a discount for pensioners?	¿Hay descuento para jubilados? *ay dehskwehntoh pahrah hoobeelahdohs?*
Can I take (flash) photos/can I film here?	¿Se pueden sacar fotos (con flash)/ filmar aquí? *seh pwehdehn sahkahr fohtohs(kohn flahsh)/feelmahr ahkee?*
Do you have any postcards of...?	¿Venden postales de...? *behndehn pohstahlehs deh...?*
Do you have an English...?	¿Tiene un...en inglés? *tyehneh oon...ehn eenglehs?*
– an English catalogue?	¿Tiene un catálogo en inglés? *tyehneh oon kahtahlohgoh ehn eenglehs?*

– an English programme?	¿Tiene un programa en inglés? *tyehneh oon prohgrahmah ehn eenglehs?*
– an English brochure?	¿Tiene un folleto en inglés? *tyehneh oon fohlyehtoh ehn eenglehs?*

11.2 Going out

● **At the cinema** most films are dubbed in Spanish. Sometimes there are only two showings, in the evening, at 7 and 11pm. In this case advance booking is advisable.

Do you have this week's/month's entertainment guide?	¿Tiene la guía de los espectáculos de esta semana/este mes? *tyehneh lah gheeah deh lohs ehspehktahkoolohs deh ehstah sehmahnah/ehsteh mehs?*
What's on tonight?	¿Adónde podríamos ir esta noche? *ahdohndeh pohdreeahmohs eer ehstah nohcheh?*
We want to go to...	Nos gustaría ir a... *nohs goostahreeah eer ah...*
Which films are showing?	¿Qué películas dan? *keh pehleekoolahs dahn?*
What sort of film is that?	¿Qué clase de película es? *keh klahseh deh pehleekoolah ehs?*
suitable for everyone	para todos los públicos *pahrah tohdohs lohs poobleekohs*
not suitable for children	prohibido para menores de 12/16 años *proheebeedoh pahrah mehnohrehs deh dohtheh/dyehtheesehees ahnyohs*
original version	versión original *behrsyohn ohreeheenahl*
subtitled	subtitulada *soobteetoolahdah*
dubbed	doblada *dohblahdah*

Is it a continuous showing?	¿Es sesión continua? *ehs sehsyohn kohnteenooah?*
What's on at...?	¿Qué dan en...? *keh dahn ehn...?*
– the theatre?	¿Qué dan en el teatro? *keh dahn ehn ehl tehahtroh?*
– the concert hall?	¿Qué dan en la sala de conciertos? *keh dahn ehn lah sahlah deh kohnthyehrtohs?*
– the opera?	¿Qué dan en la ópera? *keh dahn ehn lah ohpehrah?*
Where can I find a good disco around here?	¿Dónde hay una buena discoteca por aquí? *dohndeh ay oonah bwehnah deeskohtehkah pohr ahkee?*
Is it for members only?	¿Hay que ser socio? *ay keh sehr sohthyoh?*
Where can I find a good cabaret club around here?	¿Dónde hay un buen cabaret por aquí? *dohndeh ay oon bwehn kahbahreh pohr ahkee?*
Is it evening wear only?	¿Hay que ir en traje de etiqueta? *ay keh eer ehn trahheh deh ehteekehtah?*
Should I/we dress up?	¿Es recomendable ir en traje de etiqueta? *ehs rehkohmehndahbleh eer ehn trahheh deh ehteekehtah?*
What time does the show start?	¿A qué hora empieza el espectáculo? *ah keh ohrah ehmpyehthah ehl ehspehktahkooloh?*
When's the next soccer match?	¿Cuándo es el próximo partido de fútbol? *kwahlndoh ehs ehl prohxeemoh pahrteedoh deh footbohl?*
Who's playing?	¿Quiénes juegan? *kyehnehs hwehgahn?*

I'd like an escort for tonight. Could you arrange that for me? — Quisiera contratar un/una acompañante para esta noche. ¿Podría hacerme una reserva?
keesyehrah kohntrahtahr oon/oonah ahkohmpahnyahnteh pahrah ehstah nohcheh. podreeah ahthehrmeh oonah rehsehrbah?

11.3 Booking tickets

Could you book some tickets for us? — ¿Podría hacernos una reserva?
pohdreeah ahthehrnohs oonah rehsehrbah?

We'd like to book... tickets/a table... — Quisiéramos...entradas/una mesa...
keesyehrahmohs...ehntrahdahs/oonah mehsah...

- tickets/seats in the stalls — Quisiéramos...entradas en la platea
keesyehrahmohs...ehntrahdahs ehn lah plahtehah

- tickets/seats on the balcony — Quisiéramos...entradas en el palco
keesyehrahmohs...ehntrahdahs ehn ehl pahlkoh

- box seats — Quisiéramos...entradas en el palco privado
keesyehrahmohs...ehntrahdahs ehn ehl pahlkoh preebahdoh

- a table at the front — Quisiéramos una mesa adelante
keesyehrahmohs oonah mehsah ahdehlahnteh

- in the middle — Quisiéramos una mesa al centro
keesyehrahmohs oonah mehsah ahl thehntroh

¿Para qué función desea reservar?	Which performance do you want to book for?
¿Qué sector prefiere?	Where would you like to sit?
No hay billetes.	Everything's sold out
Sólo quedan entradas de pie	It's standing room only
Sólo quedan entradas en el palco	We've only got balcony seats left
Sólo quedan entradas en la galería	We've only got seats left in the gallery
Sólo quedan entradas en la platea	We've only got stalls seats left
Sólo quedan entradas adelante	We've only got seats left at the front
Sólo quedan entradas atrás	We've only got seats left at the back
¿Cuántas entradas quiere?	How many seats would you like?
Tiene que retirar las entradas antes de las...	You'll have to pick up the tickets before...o'clock
¿Me permite las entradas?	Tickets, please
Este es su asiento	This is your seat

– at the back	Quisiéramos una mesa atrás *keesyehrahmohs oonah mehsah ahtrahs*
Could I book...seats for the...o'clock performance?	¿Podría reservar...entradas para la función de las...? *pohdreeah rehsehrbahr...ehntrahdahs pahrah lah foonthyohn deh lahs...?*
Are there any seats left for tonight?	¿Quedan entradas para esta noche? *kehdahn ehntrahdahs pahrah ehstah nohcheh?*
How much is a ticket?	¿Cuánto sale la entrada? *kwahntoh sahleh lah ehntrahdah?*

When can I pick the tickets up? ____ ¿Cuándo puedo pasar a retirar las entradas?
kwahndoh pwehdoh pahsahr ah rehteerahr lahs ehntrahdahs?

I've got a reservation ___ Tengo una reserva
tehngoh oonah rehsehrbah

My name's... _________ Me llamo...
meh lyahmoh...

12 Sports

12.1 Sporting questions

Where can we... around here?	¿Dónde se puede...? *dohndeh seh pwehdeh...?*
Is there a... around here?	¿Hay algún...por aquí cerca? *ay ahlgoon...pohr ahkee thehrkah?*
Can I hire a...here?	¿Alquilan...? *ahlkeelahn...?*
Can I take...lessons?	¿Dan clases de...? *dahn klahsehs deh...?*
How much is that per hour/per day/class?	¿Cuánto sale por hora/día/clase? *kwahntoh sahleh pohr ohrah/deeah/klahseh?*
Do I need a permit for that?	¿Se necesita un permiso? *seh nehthehseetah oon pehrmeesoh?*
Where can I get the permit?	¿Dónde se consiguen los permisos? *dohndeh seh kohnseeghehn lohs pehrmeesohs?*

12.2 By the waterfront

Is it a long way to the sea still?	¿Falta mucho para llegar al mar? *fahltah moochoh pahrah lyehgahr ahl mahr?*
Is there a...around here?	¿Hay algún...por aquí? *ay ahlgoon...pohr ahkee?*
– an outdoor/indoor/ public swimming pool	¿Hay alguna piscina por aquí? *ay ahlgoonah peestheenah pohr ahkee?*
– a sandy beach	¿Hay alguna playa con arena por aquí? *ay ahlgoonah plahyah kohn ahrehnah pohr ahkee?*
– a nudist beach	¿Hay alguna playa nudista por aquí? *ay ahlgoonah plahyah noodeestah pohr ahkee?*
– mooring	¿Hay algún atracadero por aquí? *ay ahlgoon ahtrahkahdehroh pohr ahkee?*

Are there any rocks here?	¿Hay rocas? *ay rohkahs?*
When's high/low tide?	¿Cuándo sube/baja la marea? *kwahndoh soobeh/bahhah lah mahrehah?*
What's the water temperature?	¿Qué temperatura tiene el agua? *keh tehmpehrahtoorah tyehneh ehl ahgwah?*
Is it (very) deep here?	¿Es (muy) profundo? *ehs mwee prohfoondoh?*
Can you stand here?	¿Se puede hacer pie? *seh pwehdeh ahthehr pyeh?*
Is it safe to swim here?	¿Es seguro para nadar? *ehs sehgooroh pahrah nahdahr?*
Are there any currents?	¿Hay corriente? *ay kohrryehnteh?*
Are there any rapids/waterfalls in this river?	¿Este río tiene rápidos/cascadas? *ehsteh reeoh tyehneh rahpeedohs/kahskahdahs?*
What does that flag/buoy mean?	¿Qué significa aquella bandera/boya? *keh seegneefeekah ahkehlyah bahndehrah/bohyah?*
Is there a life guard on duty here?	¿Hay algún vigilante de servicio? *ay ahlgoon veeheelante deh sehrbeetheeoh?*
Are dogs allowed here?	¿Está permitido traer perros? *ehstah pehrmeeteedoh trahehr pehrrohs?*
Is camping on the beach allowed?	¿Está permitido acampar en la playa? *ehstah pehrmeeteedoh ahkahmpahr ehn lah plahyah?*
Are we allowed to build a fire here?	¿Está permitido hacer fuego? *ehstah pehrmeeteedoh ahthehr fwehgoh?*

Peligro Danger	Prohibido pescar No fishing	Prohibido bañarse No swimming
Aguas de pesca Fishing water	Prohibido hacer surfing No surfing	Permiso obligatorio Permits only

12.3 In the snow

Can I take ski lessons here?	¿Dan clases de esquí? *dahn klahsehs deh eskee?*
for beginners/advanced	para principiantes/avanzados *pahrah preentheepyahntehs/ahbahnthahdohs*
How large are the groups?	¿De cuántas personas son los grupos? *deh kwahntahs pehrsohnahs sohn lohs groopohs?*
What language are the classes in?	¿En qué idioma son las clases? *ehn keh eedyohmah sohn lahs klahsehs?*
I'd like a lift pass, please	Quisiera un pase para las telesillas *keesyehrah oon pahseh pahrah lahs tehlehseelyahs*
Must I give you a passport photo?	¿Se necesita foto? *seh nehthehseetah fohtoh?*
Where can I have a passport photo taken?	¿Dónde puedo sacarme fotos? *dohndeh pwehdoh sahkahrmeh fohtohs?*
Where are the beginners' slopes?	¿Dónde están las pistas para principiantes? *dohndeh ehstahn lahs peestahs pahrah preentheepyahntehs?*
Are there any runs for cross-country skiing?	¿Hay pistas de esquí de fondo por aquí? *ay peestahs deh ehskee deh fohndoh pohr ahkee?*
Have the cross-country runs been marked?	¿Las pistas de esquí de fondo están señalizadas? *lahs peestahs deh ehskee deh fohndoh ehstahn sehnyahleethahdahs?*
Are the...in operation?	¿Están abiertos los...? *ehstahn ahbyehrtohs lohs...?*
– the ski lifts	¿Ya funcionan los telesquís? *yah foonthyohnahn lohs tehlehskees?*
– the chair lifts	¿Ya funcionan las telesillas? *yah foonthyohnahn lahs tehlehseelyahs?*
Are the slopes usable?	¿Están abiertas las pistas? *ehstahn ahbyehrtahs lahs peestahs?*

13

Sickness

13.1 Call (fetch) the doctor

Could you call/fetch a doctor quickly, please?	¿Podría llamar/ir a buscar rápido a un médico, por favor? *pohdreeah lyahmahr/eer ah booskahr rahpeedoh ah oon mehdeekoh, pohr fahbohr?*
When does the doctor have surgery?	¿Cuándo tiene consulta el médico? *kwahndoh tyehneh kohnsooltah ehl mehdeekoh?*
When can the doctor come?	¿Cuándo puede venir el médico? *kwahndoh pwehdeh behneer ehl mehdeekoh?*
I'd like to make an appointment to see the doctor	¿Podría pedirme hora con el médico? *pohdreeah pehdeermeh ohrah kohn ehl mehdeekoh?*
I've got an appointment to see the doctor at...	Tengo hora con el médico para las... *tehngoh ohrah kohn ehl mehdeekoh pahrah lahs...*
Which doctor/chemist has night/weekend duty?	¿Qué médico/farmacia está de guardia esta noche/este fin de semana? *keh mehdeekoh/fahrmahthyah ehstah deh gwahrdyah ehstah nohcheh/ehsteh feen deh sehmahnah?*

13.2 Patient's ailments

I don't feel well	No me siento bien *noh meh syehntoh byehn*
I'm dizzy	Tengo mareos *tehngoh mahrehohs*
– ill	Estoy enfermo *ehstoy ehnfehrmoh*
– sick	Tengo náuseas *tehngoh nahoosehahs*
I've got a cold	Estoy acatarrado *ehstoy ahkahtahrrahdoh*
It hurts here	Me duele aquí *meh dwehleh ahkee*
I've been throwing up	He devuelto *eh dehbwehltoh*

I've got...	Tengo molestias de... *tehngoh mohlehstyahs deh...*
I'm running a temperature of... degrees	Tengo...grados de fiebre *tehngoh...grahdohs deh fyehbreh*
I've been stung by a wasp	Me ha picado una avispa *meh ah peekahdoh oonah ahbeespah*
I've been stung by an insect	Me ha picado un insecto *meh ah peekahdoh oon eensehktoh*
I've been bitten by a dog	Me ha mordido un perro *meh ah mohrdeedoh oon pehrroh*
I've been stung by a jellyfish	Me ha picado una medusa *meh ah peekahdoh oonah mehdoosah*
I've been bitten by a snake	Me ha mordido una serpiente *meh ah mohrdeedoh oonah sehrpyehnteh*
I've been bitten by an animal	Me ha picado un insecto *meh ah peekahdoh oon eensehktoh*
I've cut myself	Me he cortado *meh eh kohrtahdoh*
I've burned myself	Me he quemado *meh eh kehmahdoh*
I've grazed myself	Tengo una rozadura *tehngoh oonah rohthahdoorah*
I've had a fall	Me he caído *meh eh kaheedoh*
I've sprained my ankle	Me he torcido el tobillo *meh eh tohrtheedoh ehl tohbeelyoh*
I've come for the morning-after pill	Vengo a que me dé una píldora del día después *behngoh ah keh meh deh oonah peeldohrah dehl deeah dehspwehs*

13.3 The consultation

Patient's medical history

I'm a diabetic	Soy diabético *soy deeahbehteekoh*
I have a heart condition	Soy enfermo cardíaco *soy ehnfehrmoh kahrdeeahkoh*

¿Qué molestias tiene?	What seems to be the problem?
¿Cuánto hace que tiene estas molestias?	How long have you had these symptoms?
¿Ha tenido estas molestias anteriormente?	Have you had this trouble before?
¿Qué temperatura tiene?	How high is your temperature?
Desnúdese	Get undressed, please
Desvístase de la cintura para arriba	Strip to the waist, please
Allí puede quitarse la ropa	You can undress there
Descúbrase el brazo izquierdo/derecho	Roll up your left/right sleeve, please
Recuéstese aquí	Lie down here, please
¿Le duele esto?	Does this hurt?
Respire hondo	Breathe deeply
Abra la boca	Open your mouth

I have asthma ________	Soy asmático *soy ahsmahteekoh*
I'm allergic to... ________	Soy alérgico a... *soy ahlehrheekoh ah...*
I'm...months pregnant __	Estoy embarazada de...meses *ehstoy ehmbahrahthadah deh...mehsehs*
I'm on a diet ________	Sigo una dieta *seegoh oonah dyehtah*
I'm on medication/ the pill _____	Tomo medicamentos/la píldora *tohmoh mehdeekahmehntohs/lah peeldohrah*
I've had a heart attack once before _	He tenido un ataque cardíaco anteriormente *eh tehneedoh oon ahtahkeh kahrdeeahkoh ahntehryohrmehnteh*
I've had a(n)... operation ________	Me han operado del/de la... *meh ahn ohpehrahdoh dehl/deh lah...*
I've been ill recently ____	He estado enfermo hace poco *eh ehstahdoh ehnfehrmoh ahtheh pohkoh*
I've got an ulcer _______	Tengo una úlcera *tehngoh oonah oolthehrah*
I've got my period _____	Tengo la regla *tehngoh lah rehglah*

¿Padece alguna alergia?	Do you have any allergies?
¿Toma medicamentos?	Are you on any medication?
¿Sigue alguna dieta?	Are you on a diet?
¿Está embarazada?	Are you pregnant?
¿Está vacunado/a contra el tétanos?	Have you had a tetanus injection?

The diagnosis

Is it contagious?	¿Es contagioso? *ehs kohntahhyohsoh?*
How long do I have to stay...?	¿Hasta cuándo tengo que...? *ahstah kwahndoh tehngoh keh...?*
– in bed	¿Hasta cuándo tengo que guardar cama? *ahstah kwahndoh tehngoh keh gwahrdahr kahmah?*
– in hospital	¿Hasta cuándo tengo que quedarme en el hospital? *ahstah kwahndoh tehngoh keh kehdahrmeh ehn ehl ohspeetahl?*
Do I have to go on a special diet?	¿Tengo que seguir alguna dieta? *tehngoh keh sehgheer ahlgoonah dyehtah?*
Am I allowed to travel?	¿Puedo viajar? *pwehdoh byahhahr?*
Can I make a new appointment?	¿Puedo volver a pedir hora? *pwehdoh bohlbehr ah pehdeer ohrah?*
When do I have to come back?	¿Cuándo tengo que volver? *kwahndoh tehngoh keh bohlbehr?*
I'll come back tomorrow	Vuelvo mañana *bwehlboh mahnyahnah*

Vuelva mañana/dentro de...días	Come back tomorrow/in...days' time

No es nada grave	It's nothing serious
Se ha fracturado el/la...	Your...is broken
Se ha contusionado el/la...	You've got a/some bruised...
Se ha desgarrado el/la...	You've got (a) torn...
Tiene una inflamación	You've got an inflammation
Tiene apendicitis	You've got appendicitis
Tiene bronquitis	You've got bronchitis
Tiene una enfermedad venérea	You've got a venereal disease
Tiene gripe	You've got the flu
Ha tenido un ataque al corazón	You've had a heart attack
Tiene una infección virósica/ bacteriana	You've got an infection (viral..., bacterial...)
Tiene una pulmonía	You've got pneumonia
Tiene una úlcera	You've got an ulcer
Se ha distendido un músculo	You've pulled a muscle
Tiene una infección vaginal	You've got a vaginal infection
Tiene una intoxicación alimenticia	You've got food poisoning
Tiene una insolación	You've got sunstroke
Es alérgico a...	You're allergic to...
Está embarazada	You're pregnant
Quisiera hacerle un análisis de sangre/de orina/de materia fecal	I'd like to have your blood/urine/stools tested
Hay que suturar la herida	It needs stitching
Lo/la voy a derivar a un especialista/a un hospital	I'm referring you to a specialist/ sending you to hospital
Tiene que hacerse radiografías	You'll need to have some x-rays taken
Vuelva a tomar asiento en la sala de espera	Could you wait in the waiting room, please?
Hay que operarlo/operarla	You'll need an operation

13.4 Medication and prescriptions

Voy a recetarle unos antibióticos/un jarabe/un calmante/ unos analgésicos	I'm prescribing antibiotics/a mixture/a tranquillizer/pain killers
Tiene que guardar reposo	Have lots of rest
No tiene que salir a la calle	Stay indoors
Tiene que guardar cama	Stay in bed

antes de cada comida before meals
cápsulas capsules
diluir en agua dissolve in water
gotas drops
cada...horas every...hours
seguir la cura hasta el final finish the course
durante...días for...days
inyecciones injections
para uso externo exclusivamente not for internal use
ungüento ointment
aplicar/embadurnar rub on
cucharadas (soperas/ cucharaditas) spoonfuls (tablespoons/tea-spoons)
tragar entero swallow whole
tabletas tablets
tomar/ingerir take
estos medicamentos afectan la capacidad de conducir this medication impairs your driving
...vez/veces cada 24 horas ...times a day

How do I take this medicine?	¿Cómo se toman estos medicamentos? *kohmoh seh tohmahn ehstohs mehdeekahmehntohs?*
How many capsules/drops/injections/spoonfuls/tablets each time?	¿Cuántas cápsulas/gotas/inyecciones/cucharadas/tabletas por vez? *kwahntahs kahpsoolahs/gohtahs/eenyehkthyohnehs/koochahrahdahs pohr behth?*

How many times a day?	¿Cuántas veces al día? *kwahntahs behthehs ahl deeah?*
I've forgotten my medication. At home I take...	Se me ha olvidado traer los medicamentos. En casa tomo... *seh meh ah olbeedahdoh trahehr lohs mehdeekahmehntohs. ehn kahsah tohmoh...*
Could you make out a prescription for me?	¿Podría hacerme una receta? *pohdreeah ahthehrmeh oonah rehthehtah?*

13.5 At the dentist's

Do you know a good dentist?	¿Me podría recomendar un buen dentista? *meh pohdreeah rehkohmehndahr oon bwehn dehnteestah?*
Could you make a dentist's appointment for me? It's urgent	¿Me podría pedir hora con el dentista? Es urgente *meh pohdreeah pehdeer ohrah kohn ehl dehnteestah? ehs oorhehnteh*
Can I come in today, please?	¿Me podría atender hoy mismo? *meh pohdreeah ahtehndehr oy meesmoh?*
I have (terrible) toothache	Tengo (un terrible) dolor de muelas *tehngoh (oon tehrreebleh) dohlohr deh mwehlahs*
Could you prescribe/ give me a painkiller?	¿Me podría recetar/dar un analgésico? *meh pohdreeah rehthehtahr/dahr oon ahnahlhehseekoh?*
A piece of my tooth has broken off	Se me ha caído un pedazo de un diente *seh meh ah kaheedoh oon pehdahthoh deh oon dyehnteh*
My filling's come out	Se me ha salido un empaste *seh meh ah sahleedoh oon ehmpahsteh*
I've got a broken crown	Se me ha roto la corona *seh meh ah rohtoh lah kohrohnah*

I'd like/I don't want a local anaesthetic	Quisiera que/no quiero que me ponga anestesia local *keesyehrah keh/noh kyehroh keh meh pohngah ahnehstehsyah lohkahl*
Can you do a makeshift repair job?	¿Me podría hacer un arreglo provisional? *meh pohdreeah ahthehr oon ahrrehgloh prohbeesyohnahl?*
I don't want this tooth pulled	No quiero que me extraiga esta muela *noh kyehroh keh meh ehxtraygah ehstah mwehlah*
My dentures are broken. Can you fix them?	Se me ha roto la dentadura postiza ¿Podría arreglármela? *seh meh ah rohtoh lah dehntahdoorah pohsteethah. pohdreeah arrehglahrmehlah?*

¿Qué diente/muela le duele?	Which tooth hurts?
Tiene un absceso	You've got an abscess
Tengo que tratarle el nervio	I'll have to do a root canal
Voy a ponerle anestesia local	I'm giving you a local anaesthetic
Tengo que empastarle/extraerle/pulirle este/esta...	I'll have to fill/pull this tooth/file this...down
Tengo que usar el torno	I'll have to drill
Abra la boca	Open wide, please
Cierre la boca	Close your mouth, please
Enjuáguese	Rinse, please
¿Le sigue doliendo?	Does it hurt still?

14 In trouble

14.1 Asking for help

Help!	¡Socorro! *sohkohrroh!*
Fire!	¡Fuego! *fwehgoh!*
Police!	¡Policía! *pohleetheeah!*
Quick!	¡Rápido! *rahpeedoh!*
Danger!	¡Peligro! *pehleegroh!*
Watch out!	¡Cuidado! *kweedahdoh!*
Stop!	¡Alto! *ahltoh!*
Be careful!	¡Cuidado! *kweedahdoh!*
Don't!	¡No, no! *noh, noh!*
Let go!	¡Suelte! *swehlteh!*
Stop that thief!	¡Al ladrón! *ahl lahdrohn!*
Could you help me, please?	¿Podría ayudarme, por favor? *pohdreeah ahyoodahrmeh, pohr fahbohr?*
Where's the police station/emergency exit/fire escape?	¿Dónde está la comisaría/la salida de emergencia/la escalera de incendios? *dohndeh ehstah lah kohmeesahreeah/lah sahleedah deh ehmehrhehnthyah/lah ehskahlehrah deh eenthehndyohs?*
Where's the nearest fire extinguisher?	¿Dónde hay un extintor? *dohndeh ay oon ehxteentohr?*
Call the fire brigade!	¡Llamen a los bomberos! *lyahmehn ah lohs bohmbehrohs!*
Call the police!	¡Llamen a la policía! *lyahmehn ah lah pohleetheeah!*
Call an ambulance!	¡Llamen a una ambulancia! *lyahmehn ah oonah ahmboolahnthyah!*
Where's the nearest phone?	¿Dónde hay un teléfono? *dohndeh ay oon tehlehfohnoh?*
Could I use your phone?	¿Podría llamar por teléfono? *pohdreeah lyahmahr pohr tehlehfohnoh?*
What's the emergency number?	¿Cuál es el número de urgencias? *kwahl ehs ehl noomehroh deh oorhehnthyahs?*

What's the number for the police? _ ¿Cuál es el número de la policía?
kwahl ehs ehl noomehroh deh lah pohleetheeah?

14.2 Loss

I've lost my purse/wallet _____ Se me ha perdido el monedero/la cartera
seh meh ah pehrdeedoh ehl mohnehdehroh/lah kahrtehrah

I left my...behind yesterday _______ Ayer me dejé el/la...
ahyehr meh dehheh ehl/lah...

I left my...here _________ Me he dejado el/la...aquí
meh eh dehhahdoh ehl/lah...ahkee

Did you find my...? _____ ¿Han encontrado mi...?
ahn ehnkohntrahdoh mee...?

It was right here _______ Estaba aquí
ehstahbah ahkee

It's quite valuable ______ Es muy valioso
ehs mwee bahlyohsoh

Where's the lost property office? _______ ¿Dónde está la oficina de objetos perdidos?
dohndeh ehstah lah ohfeetheenah deh ohbhehtohs pehrdeedohs?

14.3 Accidents

There's been an accident _______ Ha habido un accidente
ah ahbeedoh oon ahktheedehnteh

Someone's fallen into the water _ Se ha caído alguien al agua
seh ah kaheedoh ahlgyehn ahl ahgwah

There's a fire _________ Hay un incendio
ay oon eenthehndyoh

Is anyone hurt? ________ ¿Hay algún herido?
ay ahlgoon ehreedoh?

Some people have been/ no one's been injured	(No) hay heridos *(noh) ay ehreedohs*
There's someone in the car/train still	Todavía queda alguien en el coche/tren *tohdahbeeah kehdah ahlgyehn ehn ehl kohcheh/trehn*
It's not too bad. Don't worry	No es grave. No se preocupe *noh ehs grahbeh. noh seh prehohkoopeh*
Leave everything the way it is, please	No toque nada *noh tohkeh nahdah*
I want to talk to the police first	Primero quisiera hablar con la policía *preemehroh keesyehrah ahblahr kohn lah pohleetheeah*
I want to take a photo first	Primero quisiera sacar una foto *preemehroh keesyehrah sahkahr oonah fohtoh*
Here's my name and address	Aquí tiene mi nombre y dirección *ahkee tyehneh mee nohmbreh ee deerehkthyohn*
Could I have your name and address?	¿Me da su nombre y dirección? *meh dah soo nohmbreh ee deerehkthyohn?*
Could I see some identification/your insurance papers?	¿Me permite su carnet de identidad/sus papeles del seguro? *meh pehrmeeteh soo kahrneh deh eedehnteedahdh/soos pahpehlehs dehl sehgooroh?*
Will you act as a witness?	¿Le importaría hacer de testigo? *leh eempohrtahreeah ahthehr deh tehsteegoh?*
I need the details for the insurance	Necesito los datos para el seguro *nehthehseetoh lohs dahtohs pahrah ehl sehgooroh*
Are you insured?	¿Está asegurado? *ehstah ahsehgoorahdoh?*
Third party or comprehensive?	¿Responsabilidad civil o contra todo riesgo? *rehspohnsahbeeleedahdh theebeel oh kohntrah tohdoh ryehsgoh?*

Could you sign here, please?	Firme aquí, por favor *feermeh ahkee, pohr fahbohr*

14.4 Theft

I've been robbed	Me han robado *meh ahn rohbahdoh*
My...has been stolen	Me han robado el/la... *meh ahn rohbahdoh ehl/lah...*
My car's been broken into	Me han abierto el coche *meh ahn ahbyehrtoh ehl kohcheh*

14.5 Missing person

I've lost my child/ grandmother	Se ha perdido mi hijo/mi hija/mi abuela *seh ah pehrdeedoh mee eehoh/mee eehah/mee ahbwehlah*
Could you help me find him/her?	¿Podría ayudarme a buscarlo/la? *pohdreeah ahyoodahrmeh ah booskahrloh/lah?*
Have you seen a small child?	¿Ha visto a un niño pequeño/a una niña pequeña? *ah veestoh ah oon neenyoh pehkehnyoh/ah oonah neenyah pehkehnyah?*
He's/she's...years old	Tiene...años *tyehneh...ahnyohs*
He's/she's got short/long/blond/red/ brown/black/ grey/curly/ straight/frizzy hair	Tiene el pelo corto/largo/rubio/rojo/castaño/negro/ canoso/rizado/liso/crespo *tyehneh ehl pehloh/ kohrtoh /lahrgoh/roobyoh/kahstahnyoh/neh groh/kahnohsoh/reethahdoh/leesoh/krehs poh*
with a ponytail	con cola de caballo *kohn kohlah deh kahbahlyoh*

with plaits	con trenzas *kohn trehnthahs*
in a bun	con moño *kohn mohnyoh*
He's/she's got blue/brown/green eyes	Tiene ojos azules/marrones/verdes *tyehneh ohhohs ahthoolehs/mahrrohnehs/behrdehs*
He's wearing swimming trunks/ mountaineering boots	Lleva bañador/botas de montaña *lyehbah bahnyahdohr/bohtahs deh mohntahnyah*
with/without glasses/ a bag	con/sin gafas/bolso *kohn/seen gahfahs/bohlsoh*
tall/short	alto/bajito *ahltoh/bahheetoh*
This is a photo of him/her	Esta es su foto *ehstah ehs soo fohtoh*
He/she must be lost	Seguramente se habrá perdido *sehgoorahmehnteh seh ahbrah pehrdeedoh*

14.6 The police

An arrest

Los papeles del coche, por favor	Your registration papers, please
Conducía demasiado rápido	You were speeding
Tiene mal aparcado el coche	You're not allowed to park here
No ha puesto monedas en el parquímetro	You haven't put money in the meter
No le funcionan los faros	Your lights aren't working
Le vamos a poner una multa de...euros	That's a...euros fine
¿Va a pagar la multa en el acto?	Do you want to pay on the spot?
Tiene que pagar en el acto	You'll have to pay on the spot

I don't speak Spanish	No hablo español *noh ahbloh ehspahnyohl*
I didn't see the sign	No he visto el cartel *noh eh beestoh ehl kahrtehl*
I don't understand what it says	No entiendo lo que dice *noh ehntyehndoh loh keh deetheh*
I was only doing... kilometres an hour	Sólo iba a...kilómetros por hora *sohloh eebah ah...keelohmehtrohs pohr ohrah*
I'll have my car checked	Haré revisar el coche *ahreh rehbeesahr ehl kohcheh*
I was blinded by oncoming lights	Me cegó un coche que venía de frente *meh thehgoh oon kohcheh keh behneeah deh frehnteh*

At the police station

I want to report a collision/missing person/rape	Vengo a hacer la denuncia de un choque/un extravío/una violación *behngoh ah ahthehr lah dehnoonthyah deh oon chohkeh/oon ehxtrahbeeoh/oonah beeohlahthyohn*
Could you make out a report, please?	¿Podría hacer un atestado? *pohdreeah ahthehr oon ahtehstahdoh?*
Could I have a copy for the insurance?	¿Me podría dar una copia para el seguro? *meh pohdreeah dahr oonah kohpyah pahrah ehl sehgooroh?*
I've lost everything	He perdido todo *eh pehrdeedoh tohdoh*
I'd like an interpreter	Quisiera un intérprete *keesyehrah oon eentehrprehteh*
I'm innocent	Soy inocente *soy eenohthehnteh*
I don't know anything about it	No sé nada *noh seh nahdah*

I want to speak to someone...	Quisiera hablar con alguien de... *keesyehrah ahblahr kohn ahlgyehn deh...*
from the British consulate	Quisiera hablar con alguien del Consulado Británico *keesyehrah ahblahr kohn ahlgyehn dehl kohnsoolahdoh breetahneekoh*
I need to see someone from the British embassy	Quisiera hablar con alguien de la Embajada Británica *keesyehrah ahblahr kohn ahlgyehn deh lah ehmbahhahdah breetahneekah*
I want a lawyer who speaks English	Quisiera un abogado que hable inglés *keesyehrah oon ahbohgahdoh keh ahbleh eenglehs*

¿Dónde ha sido?	Where did it happen?
¿Qué se le ha perdido?	What's missing?
¿Qué le han robado?	What's been taken?
¿Me permite su documento de identidad?	Could I see some identification?
¿A qué hora ocurrió?	What time did it happen?
¿Quiénes estuvieron implicados?	Who was involved?
¿Hay testigos?	Are there any witnesses?
Rellene este formulario	Fill this out, please
Firme aquí, por favor	Sign here, please
¿Quiere un intérprete?	Do you want an interpreter?

15 Word list and Basic grammar

Word list English – Spanish

● **This word list** is meant to supplement the previous chapters. Nouns are always accompanied by the Spanish definite article in order to indicate whether it is a masculine (el) or feminine (la) word. In a number of cases, words not contained in this list can be found elsewhere in this booklet, namely in the lists of the parts of the car, the bicycle and the tent. Many food terms can be found in the Spanish-English list in 4.7.

A

a little	un poco	*oon pohkoh*
above (up)	arriba	*ahrreebah*
abroad	el extranjero	*ehl ehxtrahnhehroh*
accident	el accidente	*ehl ahktheedehnteh*
adder	la víbora	*la veebohrah*
addition	la suma	*lah soomah*
address	la dirección	*lah deerehkthyohn*
admission	la entrada	*lah ehntrahdah*
admission price	el precio de entrada	*ehl prehthyoh deh lah ehntrahdah*
admission ticket	la entrada	*lah ehntrahdah*
advice	el consejo	*ehl kohnsehhoh*
after	después de	*dehspwehs deh*
afternoon (in the)	(por) la tarde	*(pohr) lah tahrdeh*
aftershave	la loción para después del afeitado	*lah lohthyohn pahrah dehspwehs dehl ahfehytahdoh*
again	de nuevo	*deh nwehboh*
against	contra	*kohntrah*
age	la edad	*lah ehdahdh*
Aids	el Sida	*ehl seedah*
air conditioning	el aire acondicionado	*ehl ayreh ahkohndeethyohnahdoh*
air mattress	el colchón neumático	*ehl kohlchohn nehoomahteekoh*

aircraft	el avión	*ehl ahbyohn*
airport	el aeropuerto	*ehl ahehrohpwehrtoh*
alarm	la alarma	*lah ahlahrmah*
alarm clock	el despertador	*ehl dehspehrtahdohr*
alcohol	el alcohol	*ehl ahlkohohl*
all the time	cada vez	*kahdah behth*
allergic	alérgico	*ahlehrheekoh*
alone	solo	*sohloh*
always	siempre	*syehmpreh*
ambulance	la ambulancia	*lah ahmboolahnthyah*
amount	el importe	*ehl eempohrteh*
amusement park	el parque de atracciones	*ehl pahrkeh deh ahtrahkthyohnehs*
anaesthetize	anestesiar	*ahnehstehsyahr*
anchovy	la anchoa	*lah ahnchohah*
angry	enfadado	*ehnfahdahdoh*
animal	el animal	*ehl ahneemahl*
ankle	el tobillo	*ehl tohbeelyoh*
answer	la respuesta	*lah rehspwehstah*
ant	la hormiga	*lah ohrmeegah*
antibiotics	los antibióticos	*lohs ahnteebyohteekohs*
antifreeze	el anticongelante	*ehl ahnteekohnhehlahnteh*
antique	antiguo	*ahnteegwoh*
antiques	las antigüedades	*lahs ahnteegwehdahdehs*
anus	el ano	*ehl ahnoh*
apartment	el apartamento	*ehl ahpahrtahmehntoh*
aperitif	el aperitivo	*ehl ahpehreeteeboh*
apologies	las disculpas	*lahs deeskoolpahs*
apple	la manzana	*lah mahnthahnah*
apple juice	el zumo de manzana	*ehl thoomoh deh mahnthahnah*
apple pie	la tarta de manzana	*lah tahrtah deh mahnthahnah*
apple sauce	el puré de manzanas	*ehl pooreh deh mahnthahnahs*
appointment	la hora	*lah ohrah*
approximately	más o menos	*mahs oh mehnohs*

April	abril	*ahbreel*
archbishop	el arzobispo	*ehl ahrthohbeespoh*
architecture	la arquitectura	*lah ahrkeetehktoorah*
area	los alrededores	*lohs ahlrehdehdohrehs*
arm	el brazo	*ehl brahthoh*
arrange to meet	quedar	*kehdahr*
arrive	llegar	*lyehgahr*
arrow	la flecha	*lah flehchah*
art	el arte	*ehl ahrteh*
artery	la arteria	*lah ahrtehryah*
artichokes	las alcachofas	*lahs ahlkahchohfahs*
article	el artículo	*ehl ahrteekooloh*
artificial respiration	la respiración artificial	*lah rehspeerahthyohn ahrteefeethyahl*
arts and crafts	la artesanía	*lah ahrtehsahneeah*
ashtray	el cenicero	*ehl thehneethehroh*
ask (a question)	preguntar	*prehgoontahr*
ask for	pedir	*pehdeer*
asparagus	los espárragos	*lohs ehspahrrahgohs*
aspirin	la aspirina	*lah ahspeereenah*
assault	la agresión	*lah ahgrehsyohn*
aubergine	la berenjena	*lah behrehnhehnah*
August	agosto	*ahgohstoh*
automatic	automático	*ahootohmahteekoh*
automatic car	el coche con cambio automático	*ehl kohcheh kohn kahmbyoh ahootohmahteekoh*
autumn	el otoño	*ehl ohtohnyoh*
avalanche	el alud	*ehl ahloodh*
awake (adj.)	despierto	*dehspyehrtoh*
awning	el toldo	*ehl tohldoh*

B

baby	el bebé	*ehl behbeh*
baby food	la comida para bebés	*lah kohmeedah pahrah behbehs*

babysitter	la niñera	*lah neenyehrah*
back (at the)	atrás	*ahtrahs*
back	la espalda	*lah ehspahldah*
backpack	la mochila	*lah mohcheelah*
bacon	el tocino	*ehl tohtheenoh*
bad	mal, malo	*mahl, mahloh*
bag	la bolsa	*lah bohlsah*
baker	la panadería	*lah pahnahdehreeah*
balcony (theatre)	el palco (alto)	*ehl pahlkoh (ahltoh)*
balcony (to building)	el balcón	*ehl bahlkohn*
ball	la pelota	*lah pehlohtah*
ballet	el ballet	*ehl bahleh*
ballpoint pen	el bolígrafo	*ehl bohleegrahfoh*
banana	el plátano	*ehl plahtahnoh*
bandage	la gasa	*lah gahsah*
bank (river)	la orilla	*lah ohreelyah*
bank	el banco	*ehl bahnkoh*
bank card	la tarjeta del banco	*lah tahrhehtah dehl bahnkoh*
bar (café)	el bar	*ehl bahr*
bar (drinks' cabinet)	la barra	*lah bahrrah*
bar	la barra	*lah bahrrah*
barbecue	la barbacoa	*lah bahrbahkohah*
basketball	el baloncesto	*ehl bahlohnthehstoh*
bath	el baño	*ehl bahnyoh*
bath attendant	el bañista	*ehl bahnyeestah*
bath foam	el gel de baño	*ehl hehl deh bahnyoh*
bath towel	la toalla de baño	*lah tohahlyah deh bahnyoh*
bathing cap	el gorro de baño	*ehl gohrroh deh bahnyoh*
bathing cubicle	la caseta	*lah kahsehtah*
bathing suit	el bañador	*ehl bahnyahdohr*
bathroom	el cuarto de baño	*ehl kwahrtoh deh bahnyoh*
battery (car)	la batería	*lah bahtehreeah*
battery	la pila	*lah peelah*
beach	la playa	*lah plahyah*
beans	las judías blancas	*lahs hoodeeahs blahnkahs*
beautiful	bonito	*bohneetoh*
beauty parlour	el salón de belleza	*ehl sahlohn deh behlyehthah*

bed	la cama	*lah kahmah*
bee	la abeja	*lah ahbehhah*
beef	la carne de vaca	*lah kahrneh deh bahkah*
beer	la cerveza	*lah thehrbehthah*
beetroot	la remolacha	*lah rehmohlahchah*
begin	empezar	*ehmpehthahr*
beginner	el principiante	*ehl preentheepyahnteh*
behind	atrás	*ahtrahs*
Belgian (f)	la belga	*lah behlgah*
Belgian (m)	el belga	*ehl behlgah*
Belgium	Bélgica	*behlheekah*
bellboy	el mozo de cuerda	*ehl mohthoh deh kwehrdah*
belt	el cinturón	*ehl theentoorohn*
berth	la litera	*lah leetehrah*
better	mejor	*mehhohr*
bicarb	el bicarbonato	*ehl beekahrbohnahtoh*
bicycle	la bicicleta	*lah beetheeklehtah*
bicycle pump	el inflador	*ehl eenflahdohr*
bicycle repairman	el mecánico de bicicletas	*ehl mehkahneekoh deh beetheeklehtahs*
bikini	el bikini	*ehl beekeenee*
bill	la cuenta	*lah kwehntah*
billiards, to play	el juego de billar	*ehl hwehgoh deh beelyahr*
birthday (to have a)	cumplir años	*koompleer ahnyohs*
birthday	el cumpleaños	*ehl koomplehahnyohs*
biscuit	la galleta	*lah gahlyehtah*
bite	morder	*mohrdehr*
bitter	amargo	*ahmahrgoh*
black	negro	*nehgroh*
bland	soso	*sohsoh*
blanket	la manta	*lah mahntah*
bleach	teñir de rubio	*tehnyeer deh roobyoh*
blister	la ampolla	*lah ahmpohlyah*
blond	rubio	*roobyoh*
blood	la sangre	*lah sahngreh*
blood pressure	la tensión sanguínea	*lah tehnsyohn sahngheenehah*

blouse	la blusa	*lah bloosah*
blow dry	secar a mano	*sehkahr ah mahnoh*
blue	azul	*ahthool*
boat	el barco	*ehl bahrkoh*
body	el cuerpo	*ehl kwehrpoh*
boiled	cocido	*kohtheedoh*
boiled ham	el jamón de York	*ehl hahmohn deh yohrk*
bonbon	el bombón	*ehl bohmbohn*
bone	el hueso	*ehl wehsoh*
bonnet	el capó	*ehl kahpoh*
book (verb)	reservar	*rehsehrbahr*
book	el libro	*ehl leebroh*
booked	reservado	*rehsehrbahdoh*
booking office	la taquilla	*lah tahkeelyah*
bookshop	la librería	*lah leebrehreeah*
border	la frontera	*lah frohntehrah*
bored (be)	aburrirse	*ahboorreerseh*
boring	aburrido	*ahboorreedoh*
born	nacido	*nahtheedoh*
botanical gardens	el jardín botánico	*ehl hahrdeen bohtahneekoh*
both	ambos/ambas	*ahmbohs/ahmbahs*
bottle (baby's)	el biberón	*ehl beebehrohn*
bottle	la botella	*lah bohtehlyah*
bottle-warmer	el calentador de biberones	*ehl kahlehntahdohr de beebehrohnehs*
box (in theatre)	el palco	*ehl pahlkoh*
box	la caja	*kahhah*
boy	el chico	*ehl cheekoh*
bra	el sujetador	*ehl soohehtahdohr*
bracelet	la pulsera	*lah poolsehrah*
braised	estofado	*ehstohfahdoh*
brake	el freno	*ehl frehnoh*
brake fluid	el líquido de frenos	*ehl leekeedoh deh frehnohs*
bread	el pan	*ehl pahn*
bread roll	el panecillo	*ehl pahnehtheelyoh*
breakdown recovery	el auxilio en carretera	*ehl ahooxeelyoh ehn kahrrehtehrah*

break (limb)	fracturarse	*frahktoorahrseh*
breakfast	el desayuno	*ehl dehsahyoonoh*
breast	el pecho	*ehl pehchoh*
bridge	el puente	*ehl pwehnteh*
bring	llevar	*lyehbahr*
brochure	el folleto	*ehl fohlyehtoh*
broken	roto, estropeado	*rohtoh, ehstrohpehahdoh*
broth	el caldo	*ehl kahldoh*
brother	el hermano	*ehl ehrmahnoh*
brown	marrón	*mahrrohn*
bruise (verb)	contusionarse	*kohntoosyohnahrseh*
brush	el cepillo	*ehl thehpeelyoh*
Brussels sprouts	las coles de Bruselas Bruselas	*lahs kohlehs deh broosehlahs*
bucket	el cubo	*ehl kooboh*
bug	el bicho	*ehl beechoh*
building	el edificio	*ehl ehdeefeethyoh*
bullfight	la corrida de toros	*lah kohrreedah deh tohrohs*
buoy	la boya	*lah boyah*
burglary	el robo en una casa	*ehl rohboh ehn oonah kahsah*
burn (verb)	quemar	*kehmahr*
burn	la quemadura	*lah kehmahdoorah*
burnt	quemado	*kehmahdoh*
bus	el autobús	*ehl ahootohboos*
bus station	la estación de autobuses	*lah ehstahthyohn deh ahootohboos*
bus stop	la parada de autobús	*lah pahrahdah deh ahootohboos*
business class	la clase preferente	*lah klahseh prehfehrehnteh*
business trip	el viaje de negocios	*ehl byahheh deh nehgohthyohs*
busy (crowded)	hay mucha gente	*ay moochah hehnteh*
butane camping gas	el gas butano	*ehl gahs bootahnoh*
butcher's	la carnicería	*lah kahrneethehreeah*
butter	la mantequilla	*lah mahntehkeelyah*

button	el botón	*ehl bohtohn*
buy	comprar	*kohmprahr*
by airmail	el correo aéreo/ vía aérea	*ehl kohrrehoh ahehrehoh/beeah ahehrehah*

C

cabbage	la col, la berza	*lah kohl, lah behrthah*
cabin	la cabaña	*lah kahbahnyah*
cake	el pastel	*ehl pahstehl*
cake shop	la pastelería, la confitería	*lah pahstehlehreeah, lah kohnfeetehreeah*
call (by phone)	llamar por teléfono	*lyahmahr pohr tehlehfohnoh*
called, to be	llamarse	*lyahmahrseh*
camera	la máquina fotográfica	*lah mahkeenah fohtohgrahfeekah*
camp	acampar	*ahkahmpahr*
camp shop	la tienda del camping	*lah tyehndah dehl kahmpeen*
camp site	el camping	*ehl kahmpeen*
camper van	el autocaravana	*ehl ahootohkahrah-bahnah*
campfire	la fogata	*lah fohgahtah*
camping guide	la guía de camping	*lah gheeah deh kahmpeen*
camping permit	el permiso de acampar	*ehl pehrmeesoh deh ahkahmpahr*
canal boat	el barco de excursión	*ehl bahrkoh deh ehxkoorsyohn*
cancel	cancelar	*kahnthehlahr*
candle	la vela	*lah behlah*
canoe	la piragua	*lah peerahgwah*
canoeing	el piragüismo	*ehl peerahgweesmoh*
cap (hat)	el gorro	*ehl gohrroh*
car	el coche	*ehl kohcheh*
car deck	la bodega para coches	*lah bohdehgah pahrah kohchehs*
car documents	los papeles del coche	*lohs pahpehlehs dehl kohcheh*

car registration	el permiso de circulación	*ehl pehrmeesoh deh theerkoolahthyohn*
car trouble	la avería	*lah ahbehreeah*
carafe	la jarra	*lah hahrrah*
caravan	la caravana	*lah kahrahbahnah*
cardigan	el chaleco	*ehl chahlehkoh*
careful	con cuidado	*kohn kweedahdoh*
carrot	la zanahoria	*lah thahnahohryah*
carton	el cartón	*ehl kahrtohn*
cascade	la cascada	*lah kahskahdah*
cash desk	la caja	*lah kahhah*
casino	el casino	*ehl kahseenoh*
cassette	la cassette	*lah kahseht*
castle	el castillo	*ehl kahsteelyoh*
cat	el gato	*ehl gahtoh*
catalogue	el catálogo	*ehl kahtahlohgoh*
cathedral	la catedral	*lah kahtehdrahl*
cauliflower	la coliflor	*lah kohleeflohr*
cave	la gruta	*lah grootah*
CD	el compact disc	*ehl kohmpahkt deesk*
celebrate	celebrar una fiesta	*thehlehbrahr oonah fyehsta*
cellotape	la celo	*lah thehloh*
cemetery	el cementerio	*ehl thehmehntehryoh*
centimetre	centímetro(s)	*thehnteemehtroh(s)*
central heating	la calefacción central	*lah kahlehfakthyohn thehntrahl*
centre (in the)	en el centro/ medio	*ehn ehl thehntroh/mehdyoh*
centre	el centro	*ehl thehntroh*
chair	la silla	*lah seelyah*
chambermaid	la camarera	*lah kahmahrehrah*
chamois	la gamuza	*lah gahmoothah*
champagne	el champán/el cava	*ehl chahmpahn/ehl kahbah*
change (from paying)	la vuelta	*lah bwehltah*
change (train/plane)	hacer trasbordo	*ahthehr trahsbohrdoh*
change (verb)	cambiar	*kahmbyahr*
change the baby's nappy	cambiar los pañales	*kahmbyahr lohs pahnyahlehs*

change the oil	cambiar el aceite	*kahmbyahr ehl ahtheyteh*
chapel	la capilla	*lah kahpeelyah*
charter flight	el vuelo chárter	*ehl bwehloh chahrtehr*
chat up	ligar	*leegahr*
check (verb)	controlar	*kohntrohlahr*
check in	facturar	*frahktoorahr*
cheers	salud	*sahloodh*
cheese (tasty, mild)	el queso (añejo, blando)	*ehl kehsoh (ahnyehhoh,blahndoh)*
chef	el jefe	*ehl hehfeh*
chemist	la droguería	*lah drohguehreeah*
	el cheque	*ehl chehkeh*
cherries	las cerezas	*lahs thehrehthahs*
chess (play)	jugar al ajedrez	*hoogahr ahl ahehdreth*
chewing gum	el chicle	*ehl cheekleh*
chicken	el pollo	*ehl pohlyoh*
chicory	las endivias	*lahs ehndeebyahs*
child	el hijo, el niño	*ehl eehoh, ehl neenyoh*
child seat	el asiento para niños	*ehl ahsyehntoh pahrah neenyohs*
child's seat	el sillín para niños	*ehl seelyeen pahrah neenyohs*
chilled	refrigerado	*rehfreehehrahdoh*
chin	la barbilla	*lah bahrbeelyah*
chips/crisps	las patatas fritas	*lahs pahtahtahs freetahs*
chocolate	el chocolate	*ehl chohkohlahteh*
choose	elegir/escoger	*ehlehheer/ehskohhehr*
chop	la chuleta	*la choolehtah*
christian name	el nombre	*ehl nohmbreh*
church	la iglesia	*lah eeglehsyah*
church service	el servicio religioso	*ehl sehrbeethyoh rehleehyohsoh*
cigar	el puro	*ehl pooroh*
cigar shop	el estanco	*ehl ehstahnkoh*
cigarette	el cigarrillo	*ehl theegahrreelyoh*
cigarette paper	el papel de fumar	*ehl pahpehl deh foomahr*
cine camera	la filmadora	*lah feelmahdohrah*

circle	el círculo	*ehl theerkooloh*
circus	el circo	*ehl theerkoh*
city map	el plano	*ehl plahnoh*
classic/classical	clásica	*klahseekah*
clean (adj.)	limpio	*leempyoh*
clean (verb)	limpiar	*leempyahr*
clear (adj.)	claro	*klahroh*
clearance	la liquidación	*lah leekeedahthyohn*
closed	cerrado	*thehrrahdoh*
closed off	(la carretera) cerrada	*(lah kahrrehtehrah) thehrrahdah*
clothes	la ropa	*lah rohpah*
clothes hanger	la percha	*lah pehrchah*
clothes peg	la pinza para la ropa	*lah peenthah pahrah lah rohpah*
coat	el abrigo	*ehl ahbreegoh*
cockroach	la cucaracha	*lah kookahrahchah*
cod	el bacalao (fresco)	*ehl bahkahlahoh (frehskoh)*
coffee	el café	*ehl kahfeh*
coffee creamer	la crema para el café	*lah krehmah pahrah ehl kahfeh*
coffee filter	el filtro de café	*ehl feeltroh deh kahfeh*
cognac	el coñac	*ehl kohnyah*
cold	frío	*freeoh*
cold	el constipado	*ehl kohnsteepahdoh*
cold cuts	los fiambres	*lohs fyahmbrehs*
collarbone	la clavícula	*lah klahbeekoolah*
colleague	el/la colega	*ehl/lah kohlehgah*
collision	el choque	*ehl chohkeh*
cologne	el agua de tocador	*ehl ahgwah deh tohkahdohr*
colour	el color	*ehl kohlohr*
colour TV	el televisor color	*ehl tehlehbeesohr kohlohr*
coloured pencils	los lápices de colores	*lohs lahpeethehs deh kohlohrehs*
colouring book	el libro para colorear	*ehl leebroh pahrah kohlohrehahr*
comb	el peine	*ehl peheeneh*

come	venir	*behneer*
compartment	el compartimiento	*ehl kohmpahrteemyehntoh*
complaint (medical)	la molestia	*lah mohlehstyah*
complaint	la queja	*lah kehhah*
complaints book	el libro de reclamaciones	*ehl leebroh deh rehklahmahthyohnehs*
completely	del todo	*dehl tohdoh*
compliment	el cumplido	*ehl koompleedoh*
compulsory	obligatorio	*ohbleegahtohryoh*
concert	el concierto	*ehl kohnthyehrtoh*
concert hall	la sala de conciertos	*lah sahlah deh kohnthyehrtohs*
concussion	la conmoción cerebral	*lah kohnmohthyohn thehrehbrahl*
condiments	los condimentos	*lohs kohndeemehntohs*
condom	el condón	*ehl kohndohn*
congratulate	felicitar	*fehleetheetahr*
connection	el enlace	*ehl ehnlahtheh*
constipation	el estreñimiento	*ehl ehstrehnyeemyehntoh*
consulate	el consulado	*ehl kohnsoolahdoh*
consultation	la consulta	*lah kohnsooltah*
contact lens	la lentilla	*lah lehnteelyah*
contact lens solution	el líquido para las lentillas	*ehl leekeedoh pahrah lahs lehnteelyahs*
contagious	contagioso	*kohntahhyohsoh*
contest	el concurso	*ehl kohnkoorsoh*
contraceptive	el anticonceptivo	*ehl ahnteekohthehpteeboh*
contraceptive pill	la píldora anticonceptiva	*ah peeldohrah lahnteekohnthehpteebah*
convent	el convento	*ehl kohnbehntoh*
cook (verb)	cocinar	*kohtheenahr*
cook	el cocinero	*ehl kohtheenehroh*
copper	el cobre	*ehl kohbreh*
copy	la copia	*lah kohpyah*
corkscrew	el sacacorchos	*ehl sahkahkohrchohs*
corn flour	la maicena	*lah maythehnah*
corner	el rincón	*ehl reenkohn*

correct	correcto	*kohrrehktoh*
correspond	cartearse	*kahrtehahrseh*
corridor	el pasillo	*ehl pahseelyoh*
costume	el traje	*ehl trahheh*
cot	la cuna	*lah koonah*
cotton	el algodón	*ehl ahlgohdohn*
cotton wool	el algodón	*ehl ahlgohdohn*
cough	la tos	*lah tohs*
cough mixture	el jarabe para la tos	*ehl hahrahbeh pahrah lah tohs*
counter	el mostrador	*ehl mohstrahdohr*
country	el país	*ehl pahees*
country code	el indicativo del país	*ehl eendeekahteeboh dehl pahees*
country(side)	el campo	*ehl kahmpoh*
courgette	el calabacín	*ehl kahlahbahtheen*
course (of treatment)	la cura	*lah koorah*
cousin (f)	la prima	*lah preemah*
cousin (m)	el primo	*ehl preemoh*
crab	el cangrejo	*ehl kahngrehoh*
cream	la crema, la nata	*lah krehmah, lah nahtah*
credit card	la tarjeta de crédito	*lah tahrhehtah deh krehdeetoh*
crisps/chips	las patatas fritas	*lahs pahtahtahs freetahs*
croissant	el croissant	*ehl krwahsahn*
cross the road	cruzar la calle	*kroothahr lah kahlyeh*
cross-country run	la pista de esquí de fondo	*lah peestah deh ehskee deh fohndoh*
cross-country skiing	el esquí de fondo	*ehl ehskee deh fohndoh*
cross-country skis	los esquís de fondo	*lohs ehskees deh fohndoh*
crossing (journey)	la travesía	*lah trahbehseeah*
cry (verb)	llorar	*lyohrahr*
cubic metre(s)	metro(s) cúbico(s)	*mehtroh(s) koobeekoh(s)*
cucumber	el pepino	*ehl pehpeenoh*
cuddly toy	el animal de peluche	*ehl ahneemahl deh pehloocheh*
cuff links	los gemelos	*lohs hehmehlohs*

culottes	la falda-pantalón	*lah fahldah pahntahlohn*
cup	la taza	*lah tahthah*
curly	rizado	*reethahdoh*
current	la corriente	*lah kohrryehnteh*
cushion	el cojín	*ehl cohheen*
custard	las natillas	*lahs nahteelyahs*
customary	habitual	*ahbeetwahl*
customs	la aduana	*lah ahdwahna*
customs check	el control de aduanas	*ehl kohntrohl deh ahdwahnahs*
cut (verb)	cortar	*kohrtahr*
cutlery	los cubiertos	*lohs koobyehrtohs*
cycling	montar en bicicleta	*mohntahr ehn beetheeklehtah*

D

dairy products	los productos/ lácteos	*ohs prodooktohs lahktehohs*
damaged	dañado, estropeado	*dahnyahdoh, ehstrohpehahdoh*
dance	bailar	*bahylahr*
dandruff	la caspa	*lah kahspah*
danger	el peligro	*ehl pehleegroh*
dangerous	peligroso	*pehleegrohsoh*
dark	oscuro	*ohskooroh*
date	la cita	*lah theetah*
daughter	la hija	*lah eehah*
day	el día, las 24 horas	*ehl deeah, lahs beheenteekwahtroh ohrahs*
day before yesterday	anteayer	*ahntehahyehr*
dead	muerto	*mwehrtoh*
decaffeinated	sin cafeína	*seen kahfeheenah*
December	diciembre	*deethyehmbreh*
deck chair	el sillón de playa	*ehl seelyohn deh plahyah*
declare (customs)	declarar	*dehklahrahr*
deep	hondo	*ohndoh*
deep sea diving	el buceo	*ehl boothehoh*

degrees	los grados	*lohs grahdohs*
delay	el retraso	*ehl rehtrahsoh*
delicious	delicioso	*dehleethyohsoh*
dentist	el dentista	*ehl dehnteestah*
dentures	la dentadura postiza	*lah dehntahdoorah pohsteethah*
deodorant	el desodorante	*ehl dehsohdohrahnteh*
department	la sección	*lah sehkthyohn*
department stores	los grandes almacenes	*lohs grahndehs ahlmahthehnehs*
departure	la partida	*lah pahrteedah*
departure time	la hora de salida	*lah ohrah deh sahleedah*
depilatory cream	la crema depilatoria	*lah krehmah dehpeelahtohryah*
deposit (in)	en consigna	*ehn kohnseegnah*
deposit	la fianza	*lah fyahnzah*
dessert	el postre	*ehl pohstreh*
destination	el destino, el punto final	*ehl dehsteenoh, ehl poontoh feenahl*
develop (photos)	revelar	*rehbehlahr*
diabetic	el diabético	*ehl dyahbehteekoh*
dial (verb)	marcar	*mahrkahr*
diamond	el diamante	*ehl deeahmahnteh*
diarrhoea	la diarrea	*lah deeahrrehah*
dictionary	el diccionario	*ehl deekthyohnahryoh*
diesel	el gasóleo	*ehl gahsohlehoh*
diet	la dieta	*lah dyehtah*
difficulty	la dificultad	*lah deefeekooltahdh*
dining room	el comedor	*ehl kohmehdohr*
dining/buffet car	el coche restaurante	*ehl kohcheh rehstahoorahnteh*
dinner (to have)	cenar	*thehnahr*
dinner	la cena, la comida	*lah thehnah, lah kohmeedah*
dinner jacket	el smoking	*ehl smohkeen*
direction	la dirección	*lah deerehkthyohn*
directly	directo	*deerehktoh*
dirty	sucio	*soothyoh*

disabled person	el minusválido	*ehl meenoosbahleedoh*
disappearance	la desaparición	*lah dehsahpahreethyohn*
disco	la discoteca	*lah deeskohtehkah*
discount	el descuento	*ehl dehskwehntoh*
dish	el plato	*ehl plahtoh*
dish of the day	el plato del día	*ehl plahtoh dehl deeah*
disinfectant	el desinfectante	*ehl dehseenfehktahnteh*
distance	la distancia	*lah deestahnthyah*
distilled water	el agua destilada	*ehl ahgwah dehsteelahdah*
disturb	molestar	*mohlehstahr*
disturbance	el fallo	*ehl fahlyoh*
dive (verb)	bucear	*boothehahr*
diving	el buceo	*ehl boothehoh*
diving board	el trampolín	*ehl trahmpohleen*
diving gear	el equipo de buzo	*ehl ehkeepoh deh boothoh*
divorced	divorciado	*deebohrthyahdoh*
DIY-shop	la tienda de artículosde bricolaje	*lah tyehndah deh ahrteekoolohs deh breekohlaheh*
dizzy	mareado	*mahrehahdoh*
do (verb)	hacer	*ahthehr*
doctor	el médico	*ehl mehdeekoh*
dog	el perro	*ehl pehrroh*
doll	la muñeca	*lah moonyehkah*
domestic	nacionales	*nahtheeohnahlehs*
done	hecho	*ehchoh*
door	la puerta	*lah pwehrtah*
double	doble	*dohbleh*
down	abajo	*ahbahhoh*
draught (to be a)	haber corriente	*ahbehr kohrryehnteh*
draughts (play)	jugar a las damas	*hoogahr ah lahs dahmahs*
dream	soñar	*sohnyahr*
dress	el vestido	*ehl behsteedoh*
dressing gown	la bata	*lah bahtah*
drink (verb)	beber	*behbehr*
drinking chocolate	el chocolate	*ehl chohkohlahteh*
drinking water	el agua potable	*ehl ahgwah pohtahbleh*

drive (verb)	ir en coche	*eer ehn kohcheh*
driver	el chófer	*ehl chohfehr*
driving licence	el permiso de conducir	*ehl pehrmeesoh deh kohndootheer*
drought	la sequía	*lah sehkeeah*
dry (verb)	secar	*sehkahr*
dry	seco	*sehkoh*
dry clean	lavar en seco	*lahbahr ehn sehkoh*
dry cleaner's	la tintorería	*lah teentohrehreeah*
dry shampoo	el champú seco	*ehl chahmpoo sehkoh*
dummy	el chupete	*ehl choopehteh*
during	durante	*doorahnteh*
during the day	de día	*deh deeah*

E

ear	la oreja	*lah ohrehhah*
ear, nose and throat (ENT) specialist	el médico de oídos	*ehl mehdeekoh deh oheedohs*
earache	el dolor de oído	*ehl dohlohr deh oheedoh*
eardrops	las gotas para los oídos	*lahs gohtahs pahrah lohs oheedohs*
early	temprano	*tehmprahnoh*
earrings	los pendientes	*lohs pehndyehntehs*
earth	la tierra	*lah tyehrrah*
earthenware	la cerámica	*lah thehrahmeekah*
east	el este	*ehl ehsteh*
easy	fácil	*fahtheel*
eat	comer	*kohmehr*
eczema	el eczema	*ehl ehkthehmah*
egg	el huevo	*ehl wehboh*
elastic band	la goma elástica	*lah gohmah ehlahsteekah*
electric	eléctrico	*ehlehktreekoh*
electricity	la corriente	*lah kohrryehnteh*
embassy	la embajada	*lah ehmbahhahdah*
emergency brake	el freno de emergencia	*ehl frehnoh deh ehmehrhehnthyah*

emergency exit	la salida de emergencia	*lah sahleedah deh ehmehrhehnthyah*
emergency number	el número de urgencias	*ehl noomehroh deh oorhehnthyahs*
emergency phone	el teléfono de emergencia	*ehl tehlehfohnoh deh ehmehrhehnthyah*
emergency triangle	el triángulo reflectante	*ehl treeahngooloh rehflehktahnteh*
emery board	la lima (para uñas)	*lah leemah (pahrah oonyahs)*
empty	vacío	*bahtheeoh*
engaged (phone)	comunicando	*kohmooneekahndoh*
engaged	ocupado	*ohkoopahdoh*
English	inglés	*eenglehs*
enjoy	disfrutar	*deesfrootahr*
entertainment guide	la guía de los espectáculos	*lah gheeah deh lohs ehspehktahkoolohs*
envelope	el sobre	*ehl sohbreh*
escort	el/la acompañante	*ehl/lah ahkohmpahnyahnteh*
evening	la tarde	*lah tahrdeh*
evening wear	el traje de etiqueta	*ehl trahheh deh ehteekehtah*
event	el acontecimiento	*ehl akohntehtheemyehntoh*
event (social)	la función	*lah foonthyohn*
everything	todo	*tohdoh*
everywhere	en todas partes	*ehn tohdahs pahrtehs*
examine	reconocer	*rehkohnohthehr*
excavation	las excavaciones	*lahs ehxkahbahthyohnehs*
excellent	excelente, estupendo	*ehxthehlehnteh, ehstoopehndoh*
exchange (verb)	cambiar	*kahmbyahr*
exchange office	la oficina de cambio	*lah ohfeetheenah deh kahmbyoh*
exchange rate	la cotización, el tipo de cambio	*lah kohteethahthyohn, ehl teepoh deh kahmbyoh*
excursion	la excursión organizada	*lah ehxkoorsyohn ohrgahneethahdah*
exhibition	la exposición	*lah ehxpohseethyohn*
exit	la salida	*lah sahleedah*

expenses	los gastos	*lohs gahstohs*
expensive	caro	*kahroh*
explain	explicar	*ehxpleekahr*
express train	el tren rápido	*ehl trehn rahpeedoh*
external	tópico, externo	*tohpeekoh, ehxtehrnoh*
eye	el ojo	*ehl ohhoh*
eye drops	las gotas para los ojos	*lahs gohtahs pahrah lohs ohhohs*
eye shadow	la sombra de ojos	*lah sohmbrah deh ohhohs*
eye specialist	el oculista	*ehl ohkooleestah*
eyeliner	el lápiz de ojos	*ehl lahpeeth deh ohhohs*

F

face	la cara	*lah kahrah*
factory	la fábrica	*lah fahbreekah*
fair	la feria	*lah fehryah*
fall	caer(se)	*kahehr(seh)*
family	la familia	*lah fahmeelyah*
famous	famoso	*fahmohsoh*
far away	lejos	*lehhohs*
farm	la granja	*lah grahnhah*
farmer	el campesino	*ehl kahmpehseenoh*
farmer's wife	la campesina	*lah kahmpehseenah*
fashion	la moda	*lah mohdah*
fast	rápido	*rahpeedoh*
father	el padre	*ehl pahdreh*
fault (blame)	la culpa	*lah koolpah*
fax (verb)	enviar un fax	*ehnbyahr oon fahx*
February	febrero	*fehbrehroh*
feel (verb)	sentir	*sehnteer*
feel like	apetecer	*ahpehtehthehr*
fence	la verja	*lah behrhah*
ferry	el transbordador	*ehl trahnsbohrdahdohr*
fever	la fiebre	*lah fyehbreh*
fill (tooth)	empastar	*ehmpahstahr*
fill out	rellenar	*rehlyehnahr*

filling	el empaste	*ehl ehmpahsteh*
film (camera)	el rollo	*ehl rohlyoh*
film	la película	*lah pehleekoolah*
filter	el filtro	*ehl feeltroh*
find (verb)	encontrar	*ehnkohntrahr*
fine	la multa	*lah mooltah*
finger	el dedo	*ehl dehdoh*
fire	el fuego	*ehl fwehgoh*
fire (house etc.)	el incendio	*ehl eenthehndyoh* fire
brigade	los bomberos	*lohs bohmbehrohs*
fire escape	la escalera de incendios	*lah ehskahlehrah deh eenthehndyohs*
fire extinguisher	el extintor	*ehl ehxteentohr*
first	primero	*preemehroh*
first aid	los primeros auxilios	*lohs preemehrohs ahooxeelyohs*
first class	la primera clase	*lah preemehrah klahseh*
fish (verb)	pescar	*pehskahr*
fish	el pescado	*ehl pehskahdoh*
fishing rod	la caña de pescar	*lah kanyah deh pehskahr*
fitness centre	el gimnasio	*ehl heemnahsyoh*
fitness training	la gimnasia	*lah heemnahsyah*
fitting room	el probador	*ehl prohbahdohr*
fix puncture	arreglar el pinchazo	*ahrrehglahr ehl peenchahthoh*
flag	la bandera	*lah bahndehrah*
flamenco	el flamenco	*ehl flahmehnkoh*
flash cube	el cuboflash	*ehl koobohflahsh*
flash gun/bulb	el flash	*ehl flahsh*
flat	el piso	*ehl peesoh*
flea market	el mercadillo, el rastro	*ehl mehrkahdeelyoh, ehl rahstroh*
flight	el vuelo	*ehl bwehloh*
flight number	el número de vuelo	*ehl noomehroh deh bwehloh*
flood	la inundación	*lah eenoondathyohn*
floor	el piso	*ehl peesoh*
flour	la harina	*lah ahreenah*

flu	la gripe	*lah greepeh*
fly (insect)	la mosca	*lah mohskah*
fly (verb)	volar	*bohlahr*
fly-over	el viaducto	*ehl beeahdooktoh*
fog	la niebla	*lah nyehblah*
foggy (be)	haber niebla	*ahbehr nyehblah*
folkloristic	folclórico	*fohlklohreekoh*
follow	seguir	*sehgeer*
food	el alimento	*ehl ahleemehntoh* food
poisoning	la intoxicación alimenticia	*lah eentohxeekaht-hyohn ahleemehnteethyah*
foodstuffs	los víveres	*lohs beebehrehs*
foot	el pie	*ehl pyeh*
for	antes, delante de	*ahntehs, dehlahnteh deh*
for hire	se alquila	*seh ahlkeelah*
forbidden	prohibido	*proheebeedoh*
forehead	la frente	*lah frehnteh*
foreign	extranjero	*ehxtrahnhehroh*
forget	olvidar	*ohlbeedahr*
fork	el tenedor	*ehl tehnehdohr*
form	el formulario	*ehl fohrmoolahryoh*
fort	la fortificación	*lah fohrteefeekahthyohn*
forward (send)	enviar	*ehnbyahr*
fountain	la fuente	*lah fwehnteh*
four-star petrol	súper	*soopehr*
frame	la montura	*lah mohntoorah*
free	libre	*leebreh*
free of charge	gratuito	*grahtweetoh*
free time	el tiempo libre	*ehl tyehmpoh leebreh*
freeze	helar	*ehlahr*
French	francés	*frahnthehs*
French bread	la barra de pan	*lah bahrrah deh pahn*
fresh	fresco	*frehskoh*
Friday	el viernes	*ehl byehrnehs*
fried	frito	*freetoh*
fried egg	el huevo al plato	*ehl wehboh ahl plahtoh*
friend	el amigo	*ehl ahmeegoh*

friendly	cordial, amable	*kohrdyahl, ahmahbleh*
frightened	miedoso	*myehdohsoh*
fringe	el flequillo	*ehl flehkeelyoh*
front (at the)	adelante	*ahdehlahnteh*
frozen goods	los productos congelados	*los prohdooktohs kohnhehlahdohs*
fruit	la fruta	*lah frootah*
fruit juice	el zumo de frutas	*ehl thoomoh deh frootahs*
frying pan	la sartén	*lah sahrtehn*
full	lleno	*lyehnoh*
fun	la diversión	*lah deebehrsyohn*

G

gallery	la galería de arte	*lah gahlehreeah deh ahrteh*
game	el juego	*el hwehgoh*
garage (for repairs)	el taller mecánico	*ehl tahlyehr mehkahneekoh*
garbage bag	la bolsa de basura	*lah bohlsah deh bahsoorah*
garden	el jardín	*ehl hahrdeen*
gastroenteritis	la gastroenteritis	*lah gahstrohehntehreetees*
gauze	la gasa esterilizada	*lah gahsah ehstehreeleethahdah*
gear (bicycle)	el cambio	*ehl kahmbyoh*
gel	el gel	*ehl hehl*
German	alemán	*ahlehmahn*
get married	casarse	*kahsahrseh*
get off	bajarse	*bahhahrse*
gift	el regalo	*ehl rehgahloh*
gilt	dorado	*dohrahdoh*
ginger	el jengibre	*ehl hehnheebreh*
girl	la chica	*lah cheekah*
girlfriend	la amiga	*lah ahmeegah*
giro card	la tarjeta de la caja postal	*lah tahrhehtah deh lah kahhah pohstahl*
giro cheque	el cheque postal	*ehl chehkeh pohstahl*
glacier	el glaciar	*ehl glahthyahr*

glass (tumbler)	el vaso	*ehl bahsoh*
glass (wine -)	la copa	*lah kohpah*
glasses	las gafas	*lahs gahfahs*
glider	el vuelo sin motor	*ehl bwehloh seen mohtohr*
glove	el guante	*ehl gwahnteh*
glue	la cola	*lah kohlah*
gnat	el mosquito	*ehl mohskeetoh*
go (verb)	ir	*eer*
go back, come back	volver	*bohlbehr*
go backwards	ir para atrás	*eer pahrah ahtrahs*
go out	salir	*sahleer*
goat's cheese	el queso de cabra	*ehl kehsoh deh kahbrah*
gold	el oro	*ehl ohroh*
golf	el golf	*ehl gohlf*
golf course	el campo de golf	*ehl kahmpoh deh gohlf*
gone	perdido	*pehrdeedoh*
good afternoon	buenas tardes (after 2pm)	*bwehnahs tahrdehs*
good evening	buenas tardes	*bwehnahs tahrdehs*
good morning	buenos días (before 2pm)	*bwehnohs deeahs*
good night	buenas noches	*bwehnahs nohchehs*
goodbye	la despedida	*lah dehspehdeedah*
gram	el gramo	*ehl grahmoh*
grandchild	el nieto	*ehl nyehtoh*
grandfather	el abuelo	*ehl ahbwehloh*
grandmother	la abuela	*lah ahbwehlah*
grape juice	el zumo de uvas	*ehl thoomoh deh oobahs*
grapefruit	el pomelo	*ehl pohmehloh*
grapes	las uvas	*lahs oobahs*
grave	la tumba	*lah toombah*
grease	la grasa	*lah grahsah*
green	verde	*behrdeh*
green card	la tarjeta verde	*lah tahrhehtah behrdeh*
greet	saludar	*sahloodahr*
grey (hair)	canoso	*kahnohsoh*
grey	gris	*grees*

grill (verb)	asar a la parrilla	*ahsahr ah lah pahreelyah*
grilled	tostado	*tohstahdoh*
grocer's	la tienda de comestibles	*lah tyehndah deh kohmehsteeblehs*
ground	la tierra	*lah tyehrrah*
group	el grupo	*ehl groopoh*
guest house	la pensión	*lah pehnsyohn*
guide (book)	la guía	*lah gueeah*
guide (person)	el/la guía	*ehl/lah gueeah*
guided tour	la visita guiada	*lah beeseetah gueeahdah*
gynaecologist	el ginecólogo	*ehl heenehkohlohgoh*

H

hair	el pelo	*ehl pehloh*
hairbrush	el cepillo para el pelo	*ehl thehpeelyoh parah ehl pehloh*
hairdresser (ladies', men's)	la peluquería (de señoras, caballeros)	*lah pehlookehreeah (deh sehnyohrahs, kahbahlyehrohs)*
hairpins	las horquillas	*lahs ohrkeelyahs*
hairspray	la laca para el pelo	*lah lahkah pahrah ehl pehloh*
half	medio, media, la mitad	*mehdyoh, mehdyah, lah meetahdh*
half full	lleno hasta la mitad	*lyehnoh ahstah lah meetahdh*
half kilo	el medio kilo	*ehl mehdyoh keeloh*
hammer	el martillo	*ehl mahrteelyoh*
hand	la mano	*lah mahnoh*
hand brake	el freno de mano	*ehl frehnoh deh mahnoh*
handbag	el bolso de mano	*ehl bohlsoh deh mahnoh*
handbag	el bolso	*ehl bohlsoh*
handkerchief	el pañuelo	*ehl pahnywehloh*
handmade	hecho a mano	*ehchoh ah mahnoh*
happy	contento	*kohntehntoh*
harbour	el puerto	*ehl pwehrtoh*
hard	duro	*dooroh*

haste	la prisa	*lah preesah*
hat	el sombrero	*ehl sohmbrehroh*
hay fever	la fiebre del heno	*lah fyehbreh dehl ehnoh*
hazelnut	la avellana	*lah ahbehlyahnah*
head	la cabeza	*lah kahbehthah*
headache	el dolor de cabeza	*ehl dohlohr deh kahbehthah*
health	la salud	*lah sahloodh*
health food shop	la tienda naturista	*lah tyehndah nahtooreestah*
hear	entender	*ehntehndehr*
hearing aid	el audífono	*ehl ahoodeefohnoh*
heart	el corazón	*ehl kohrahthohn*
heart patient	el enfermo cardíaco	*ehl ehnfehrmoh kahrdeeahkoh*
heat	calor	*kahlohr*
heater	la calefacción	*lah kahlehfahkthyohn*
heavy	pesado	*pehsahdoh*
heel	el talón	*ehl tahlohn*
heel (on shoe)	el tacón	*ehl tahkohn*
hello	hola	*ohlah*
helmet	el casco	*ehl kahskoh*
help (verb)	ayudar	*ahyoodahr*
help	la ayuda	*lah ahyoodah*
helping/portion	la ración	*lah rahthyohn*
herbal tea	la infusión	*lah eenfoosyohn*
here	aquí	*ahkee*
herring	el arenque	*ehl ahrehnkeh*
high	alto	*ahltoh*
high tide	la marea alta	*lah mahrehah ahltah*
highchair	la silla para niños	*lah seelyah pahrah neenyohs*
hiking	el excursionismo	*ehl ehxkoorsyohneesmoh*
hiking trip	la excursión a pie	*lah ehxkoorsyohn ah pyeh*
hip	la cadera	*lah kahdehrah*
hire	alquilar	*ahlkeelahr*
hitchhike	hacer autostop	*ahthehr ahootohstohp*
hobby	el hobby	*ehl hohbee*
hold-up/robbery	el asalto	*ehl ahsahltoh*
holiday (public)	el día de fiesta	*ehl deeah deh fyehstah*

holiday house	el chalet	*ehl chahleh*
holiday park	la urbanización	*lah oorbahneethahthyohn*
holidays	las vacaciones	*lahs bahkahthyohnehs*
home (at)	en casa	*ehn kahsah*
homesickness	la nostalgia	*lah nohstahlhyah*
honest	sincero	*seenthehroh*
honey	la miel	*lah myehl*
horizontal	horizontal	*oreethohntahl*
horrible	horrible	*ohrreebleh*
horse	el caballo	*ehl kahbahlyoh*
hospital	el hospital	*ehl ohspeetahl*
hospitality	la hospitalidad	*lah ohspeetahleedahdh*
hot	cálido/caluroso	*kahleedoh/kahloorohsoh*
hot (spicy)	picante	*peekahnteh*
hotel	el hotel	*ehl ohtehl*
hot-water bottle	la bolsa de agua caliente	*lah bohlsah deh ahgwah kahlyehnteh*
hour	la hora	*lah ohrah*
house	la casa	*lah kahsah*
houses of parliament	la cámara de diputados	*lah kahmahrah deh deepootahdohs*
housewife	el ama de casa	*ehl ahmah deh kahsah*
how far?	¿a qué distancia?	*ah keh deestahnthyah?*
how long?	¿cuánto tiempo?	*kwahntoh tyehmpoh?*
how much?	¿cuánto?	*kwahntoh?*
how?	¿cómo?	*kohmoh*
hunger	el hambre/el apetito	*ehl ahmbreh/ehl ahpehteetoh*
hurry	la prisa	*lah preesah*
husband	el marido	*ehl mahreedoh*
hut	el camarote	*ehl kahmahrohteh*
hyperventilation	la hiperventilación	*lah eepehrbehnteelahthyohn*

I

ice cream	el helado	*ehl ehlahdoh*
ice cubes	los cubitos de hielo	*lohs koobeetohs deh yehloh*

ice skating	el patinaje sobre hielo	*ehl pahteenahheh sohbreh yehloh*
idea	la idea	*lah eedehah*
identification card	el carnet de identidad	*ehl kahrneh deh eedehnteedahdh*
identify	identificar	*eedehnteefeekahr*
ignition key	la llave de contacto	*lah lyahbeh deh kohntahktoh*
ill	enfermo	*ehnfehrmoh*
illness	la enfermedad	*lah ehnfehrmehdahdh*
imagine	imaginarse	*eemahheenahrseh*
immediately	inmediatamente	*eenmehdyahtahmehnteh*
import duty	los derechos de aduana	*lohs dehrehchohs deh ahdwahnah*
impossible	imposible	*eempohseebleh*
in	en	*ehn*
in the evening	por la tarde	*pohr lah tahrdeh*
in the morning	por la mañana	*pohr lah mahnyahnah*
included	incluido	*eenklooeedoh*
indicate	señalar	*sehnyahlahr*
indicator	el intermitente	*ehl eentehrmeetehnteh*
inexpensive	barato	*bahrahtoh*
infection (viral -, bacterial -)	la infección (vírica, bacteriana)	*lah eenfehkthyohn (beereekah, bahktehryahnah)*
inflammation	la inflamación	*lah eenflahmahthyohn*
information	la información	*lah eenfohrmahthyohn*
information office	la oficina de información	*lah ohfeetheenah deh eenfohrmahthyohn*
injection	la inyección	*lah eenyehkthyohn*
injured	herido	*erhreedoh*
inner ear	el oído	*ehl oheedoh*
inner tube	la cámara	*lah kahmahrah*
innocent	inocente	*eenohthehnteh*
insect	el insecto	*ehl eensehktoh*
insect bite	la picadura de insecto	*lah peekahdoorah deh eensehktoh*
insect repellant	el aceite para los mosquitos	*ehl ahthehyteh pahrah lohs mohskeetohs*

inside	adentro	*ahdehntroh*
insole	la plantilla	*lah plahnteelyah*
instructions	las instrucciones	*lahs eenstrookthyohnehs*
insurance	el seguro	*ehl sehgooroh*
international	internacional	*eentehrnahthyohnahl*
interpreter	el intérprete	*ehl eentehrprehteh*
intersection/crossing	el cruce	*ehl krootheh*
introduce oneself	presentarse	*prehsehntahrseh*
invite (verb)	invitar	*eenbeetahr*
iodine	el yodo	*ehl yohdoh*
iron (metal)	el hierro	*ehl yehrroh*
iron (verb)	planchar	*plahnchahr*
iron	la plancha	*lah plahnchah*
ironing board	la tabla de planchar	*lah tahblah deh plahnchahr*
island	la isla	*lah eeslah*
it's a pleasure	de nada	*deh nahdah*
Italian	italiano	*eetahlyahnoh*
itch	la picazón	*lah peekahthohn*

J

jack	el gato	*ehl gahtoh*
jacket	la chaqueta	*lah chahkehtah*
jam	la mermelada	*lah mehrmehlahdah*
January	enero	*ehnehroh*
jaw	la mandíbula	*lah mahndeeboolah*
jellyfish	la medusa	*lah mehdoosah*
jeweller	la joyería	*lah hoyehreeah*
jewels	las alhajas	*lahs ahlahhahs*
jog (verb)	hacer footing	*ahthehr footeen*
joke	la broma	*lah brohmah*
journey	el viaje	*ehl byahheh*
juice	el zumo/el jugo	*ehl thoomoh/ehl hoogoh*
July	julio	*hoolyoh*
jump leads	el cable de arranque	*ehl kahbleh deh ahrrahnkeh*
jumper	el jersey	*ehl hehrsehee*
June	junio	*hoonyoh*

K

key	la llave	*lah lyahbeh*
kilo	el kilo	*ehl keeloh*
kilometre	kilómetro(s)	*keelohmehtroh(s)*
king	el rey	*ehl rehee*
kiss (verb)	besar	*behsahr*
kiss	el beso	*ehl behsoh*
kitchen	la cocina	*lah kohtheenah*
knee	la rodilla	*lah rohdeelyah*
knee socks	las medias cortas	*lahs mehdyahs kohrtahs*
knife	el cuchillo	*ehl koocheelyoh*
know	saber	*sahbehr*

L

lace	el encaje	*ehl ehnkahheh*
ladies'	el servicio para señoras	*ehl sehrbeethyoh pahrah sehnyohrahs*
lake	el lago	*ehl lahgoh*
lamp	la lámpara	*lah lahmpahrah*
land (verb)	aterrizar	*ahtehrreethahr*
lane	el carril	*ehl kahrreel*
language	el idioma	*ehl eedyohmah*
large	grande	*grahndeh*
last	pasado, último	*pahsahdoh, oolteemoh*
last night	anoche	*ahnohcheh*
late	tarde	*tahrdeh*
later	luego	*lwehgoh*
latest (at the)	a más tardar	*ah mahs tahrdahr*
laugh	reír	*reheer*
launderette	la lavandería (automática)	*lah lahbahndehreeah (ahootohmahteekah)*
law	el derecho	*ehl dehrehchoh*
laxative	el laxante	*ehl lahxahnteh*
leak	pinchado	*peenchahdoh*
leather	la piel, el cuero	*lah pyehl, ehl kwehroh*

leather goods	los artículos de piel	*lohs ahrteekoolohs deh pyehl*
leave (verb)	partir, salir	*pahrteer, sahleer*
leek	el puerro	*ehl pwehrroh*
left (on the)	a la izquierda	*ah lah eethkyehrdah*
left	izquierda	*eethkyehrdah*
left luggage	el depósito de equipajes	*ehl dehpohseetoh deh ehkeepahhehs*
leg	la pierna	*lah pyehrnah*
lemon	el limón	*ehl leemohn*
lemonade	la limonada prestar	*lah leemohnahdah prehstahr*
lens	el objetivo	*ehl ohbhehteeboh*
lentils	las lentejas	*lahs lehntehhahs*
less	menos	*mehnohs*
lesson	la clase	*lah klahseh*
letter	la carta	*lah kahrtah*
lettuce	la lechuga	*lah lehchoogah*
level crossing	el paso a nivel	*ehl pahsoh ah neebehl*
library	la biblioteca	*lah beeblyohtehkah*
lie	mentir	*mehnteer*
lie down	estar tumbado	*ehstahr toombahdoh*
lift (hitchhike)	el viaje (en autostop)	*ehl byahheh (ehn ahootohstohp)*
lift (in building)	el ascensor	*ehl ahsthehnsohr*
lift (ski)	el telesquí, el telesilla	*ehl tehlehskee,ehl tehlehseelyah*
light (for cigarette)	el fuego	*ehl fwehgoh*
light (not dark)	claro	*klahroh*
light (not heavy)	ligero	*leehehroh*
lighter	el mechero	*ehl mehchehroh*
lighthouse	el faro	*ehl fahroh*
lightning	el rayo	*ehl rahyoh*
like	gustar	*goostahr*
line	la línea	*lah leenehah*
linen	el hilo	*ehl eeloh*
lipstick	la barra de labios	*lah bahrrah deh lahbyohs*
liqueur	la copa	*lah kohpah*
liquorice	el regaliz	*ehl rehgahleeth*

listen	escuchar	*ehskoochahr*
literature	la literatura	*lah leetehrahtoorah*
litre	el litro	*ehl leetroh*
little	poco	*pohkoh*
live (verb)	vivir	*beebeer*
live together	vivir con otra persona	*beebeer kohn ohtrah pehrsohnah*
lobster	la langosta	*lah lahngohstah*
local	local	*lohkahl*
lock	la cerradura	*lah thehrrahdoorah*
long	largo	*lahrgoh*
look (verb)	mirar	*meerahr*
look for	buscar	*booskahr*
look up (person)	buscar	*booskahr*
lorry	el camión	*ehl kahmyohn*
lose	perder	*pehrdehr*
loss	la pérdida	*lah pehrdeedah*
lost (to get)	perderse, extraviarse	*pehrdehrseh, ehxtrahbyahrseh*
lost	extraviado, perdido	*ehxtrahbyahdoh, pehrdeedoh*
lost item	extravío	*ehxtrahbeeoh*
lost property office	los objetos perdidos	*lohs ohbhehtohs pehrdeedohs*
lotion	la loción	*lah lohthyohn*
loud	alto	*ahltoh*
love (be in - with)	estar enamorado de	*ehstahr ehnahmohrahdoh deh*
love (verb)	querer	*kehrehr*
love	el amor	*ehl ahmohr*
low	bajo	*bahhoh*
low tide	la marea baja	*lah mahrehah bahhah*
luck	la suerte	*lah swehrteh*
luggage	el equipaje	*ehl ehkeepahheh*
luggage locker	la consigna automática	*lah kohnseegnah ahootohmahteekah*

lunch	el almuerzo, la comida	*ehl ahlmwehrthoh, lah kohmeedah*
lungs	los pulmones	*lohs poolmohnehs*

M

macaroni	los macarrones	*lohs mahkahrrohnehs*
madam/Mrs	señora	*sehnyohrah*
magazine	la revista	*lah rehbeestah*
magnificent	magnífico	*mahgneefeekoh*
mail	el correo	*ehl kohrrehoh*
main post office	la oficina central de Correos	*ah ohfeetheenah thehntrahl deh kohrrehohs*
main road	la carretera principal	*lah kahrrehtehrah preentheepahl*
make an appointment	pedir hora	*pehdeer ohrah*
make love	acostarse/hacer el amor	*ahkohstahrseh/ahthehr ehl ahmohr*
makeshift	provisional(mente)	*prohbeesyohnahl (mehnteh)*
man	el hombre	*ehl ohmbreh*
manager	el encargado	*ehl ehnkahrgahdoh*
mandarin	la mandarina	*lah mahndahreenah*
manicure	la manicura	*lah mahneekoorah*
map	el mapa	*ehl mahpah*
marble	el mármol	*ehl mahrmohl*
March	marzo	*mahrthoh*
margarine	la margarina	*lah mahrgahreenah*
marina	el puerto deportivo	*ehl pwehrtoh dehpohrteeboh*
market	el mercado	*ehl mehrkahdoh*
marriage	el matrimonio	*ehl mahtreemohnyoh*
married	casado	*kahsahdoh*
mass	la misa	*lah meesah*
massage	el masaje	*ehl mahsahheh*
mat	mate	*mahteh*
matches	las cerillas	*lahs thehreelyahs*
May	mayo	*mahyoh*
maybe	quizá	*keethah*

mayonnaise	la mayonesa	*lah mahyohnehsah*
mayor	el alcalde	*ehl ahlkahldeh*
meal	la comida	*lah kohmeedah*
mean (verb)	significar	*seegneefeekahr*
meat	la carne	*lah kahrneh*
medical insurance	el seguro de enfermedad	*ehl sehgooroh deh ehnfehrmehdahdh*
medication	el medicamento	*ehl mehdeekahmehntoh*
medicine	el medicamento, la medicina	*ehl mehdeekahmehntoh, lah mehdeetheenah*
meet	conocer	*kohnohthehr*
melon	el melón	*ehl mehlohn*
membership	el ser socio	*ehl sehr sohthyoh*
menstruate	tener la regla	*tehnehr lah rehglah*
menstruation	la menstruación	*lah mehnstrooahthyohn*
menu	el menú, la carta	*ehl mehnoo, lah kahrtah*
menu of the day	el menú del día	*ehl mehnoo dehl deeah*
message	el recado/mensaje	*ehl rehkahdoh/mehnsahheh*
metal	el metal	*ehl mehtahl*
meter (taxi)	el taxímetro	*ehl tahxeemehtroh*
metre	metro(s)	*mehtroh(s)*
migraine	la jaqueca	*lah hahkehkah*
mild (tobacco)	rubio	*roobyoh*
milk	la leche	*lah lehcheh*
millimetre(s)	milímetro(s)	*meeleemehtroh(s)*
milometer	el cuentakilómetros	*ehl kwehntahkeelohmehtrohs*
mince	la carne picada	*lah kahrneh peekahdah*
mineral water	el agua mineral	*ehl ahgwah meenehrahl*
minute	el minuto	*ehl meenootoh*
mirror	el espejo	*ehl ehspehoh*
miss (person)	echar de menos	*ehchahr deh mehnohs*
missing (be)	faltar	*fahltahr*
mistake	el error, la equivocación	*ehl ehrrohr, lah ehkeebohkahthyohn*
mistaken (be)	equivocarse	*ehkeebohkahrseh*
misunderstanding	el malentendido	*ehl mahlehntehndeedoh*

mixture	el jarabe, la poción	*ehl hahrahbeh, lah pohthyohn*
mocha	el moca	*ehl mohkah*
modern art	el arte moderno	*ehl ahrteh mohdehrnoh*
molar	la muela	*lah mwehlah*
moment	el momento	*ehl mohmehntoh*
Monday	el lunes	*ehl loonehs*
money	el dinero	*ehl deenehroh*
month	el mes	*ehl mehs*
moped	el ciclomotor	*ehl theeklohmohtohr*
morning-after pill	la píldora para el día después	*lah peeldohrah pahrah ehl deeah dehspwehs*
mosque	la mezquita	*lah methkeetah*
motel	el motel	*ehl mohtehl*
mother	la madre	*lah mahdreh*
motor cross	el motocrós	*ehl mohtohkrohs*
motorbike	la moto	*lah mohtoh*
motorboat	la lancha motora	*lah lahnchah mohtohrah*
motorway	la autovía, la autopista	*lah ahootohbeeah, lah ahootohpeestah*
mountain	la montaña	*lah mohntahnyah*
mountain hut	el refugio	*ehl rehfoohyoh*
mountaineering	el montañismo	*ehl mohntahnyeesmoh*
mountaineering shoes	las botas de alpinismo	*lahs bohtahs deh ahlpeeneesmoh*
mouse	el ratón	*ehl rahtohn*
mouth	la boca	*lah bohkah*
much/many	mucho	*moochoh*
multi-storey car park	el estacionamiento	*ehl ehstahthyohnah-myehntoh*
muscle	el músculo	*ehl mooskooloh*
muscle spasms	los calambres (en los músculos)	*lohs kahlahmbrehs (ehn lohs mooskoolohs)*
museum	el museo	*ehl moosehoh*
mushrooms	las setas	*lahs sehtahs*
music	la música	*lah mooseekah*
musical show	la comedia musical	*lah kohmehdyah mooseekahl*

mussels	los mejillones	*lohs meheelyohnehs*
mustard	la mostaza	*lah mohstahthah*

N

nail (on hand)	la uña	*lah oonyah*
nail	el clavo	*ehl klahboh*
nail polish	el esmalte (para uñas)	*ehl ehsmahlteh(pahrah oonyahs)*
nail polish remover	el quitaesmalte	*ehl keetahehsmahlteh*
nail scissors	las tijeras de uñas	*lahs teehehrahs pahrah oonyahs*
naked	desnudo	*dehsnoodoh*
nappy	el pañal	*ehl pahnyahl*
nationality	la nacionalidad	*lah nahthyohnahleedahdh*
nature	la naturaleza	*lah nahtoorahlehthah*
naturism	el naturismo	*ehl nahtooreesmoh*
nauseous	con náuseas	*kohn nahoosehahs*
near	junto a	*hoontoh ah*
nearby	cerca	*thehrkah*
necessary	necesario	*nehthehsahryoh*
neck	la nuca	*lah nookah*
necklace	la cadena	*lah kahdehnah*
needle	la aguja	*lah ahoohah*
negative	el negativo	*ehl nehgahteeboh*
neighbours	los vecinos	*lohs behtheenohs*
nephew	el sobrino	*ehl sohbreenoh*
Netherlands	los Países Bajos	*lohs paheesehs bahhohs*
never	jamás/nunca	*hahmahs/noonkah*
new	nuevo	*nwehboh*
news	las noticias	*lahs nohteethyahs*
news stand	el quiosco	*ehl kyohskoh*
newspaper	el periódico	*ehl pehryohdeekoh*
next	próximo, que viene	*prohxeemoh, keh byehneh*
next to	al lado de	*ahl lahdoh deh*
nice (friendly)	amable	*ahmahbleh*
nice (to look at)	bonito, mono	*bohneetoh, mohnoh*

nice	bien, agradable	*byehn, ahgrahdahbleh*
niece	la sobrina	*lah sohbreenah*
night (at)	por la noche	*pohr lah nohcheh*
night	la noche	*lah nohcheh*
night duty	la guardia nocturna	*lah gwahrdyah nohktoornah*
nightclub	el cabaré	*ehl kahbahreh*
nightlife	la vida nocturna	*lah beedah nohktoornah*
nipple	la tetina	*lah tehteenah*
no	no	*noh*
no overtaking	la prohibición de adelantar	*lah proheebeethyohn deh ahdehlahntahr*
noise	el ruido	*ehl rooeedoh*
nonstop	sin escalas	*seen ehskahlahs*
no-one	nadie	*nahdyeh*
normal	normal, corriente	*nohrmahl, kohrryehnteh*
north	el norte	*ehl nohrteh*
nose	la nariz	*lah nahreeth*
nose bleed	la hemorragia nasal	*lah ehmohrrahhyah nahsahl*
nose drops	las gotas para la nariz	*lahs gohtahs pahrah lah nahreeth*
notepaper	el papel de escribir	*ehl pahpehl deh ehskreebeer*
nothing	nada	*nahdah*
November	noviembre	*nohbyehmbreh*
nowhere	en ninguna parte	*ehn neengoonah pahrteh*
nudist beach	la playa nudista	*lah plahyah noodeestah*
number	el número	*ehl noomehroh*
number plate	la matrícula	*lah mahtreekoolah*
nurse	la enfermera	*lah ehnfehrmehrah*
nutmeg	la nuez moscada	*lah nwehth mohskahdah*
nuts	los frutos secos	*lohs frootohs sehkohs*

October	octubre	*ohktoobreh*
of course	claro	*klahroh*
off	podrido	*pohdreedoh*
offer	ofrecer	*ohfrehthehr*

office	la oficina	*lah ohfeetheenah*
off-licence	la bodega, la tienda de vinos y licores	*lah bohdehgah, lah tyehndah deh beenohs ee leekohrehs*
oil	el aceite	*ehl ahtheyteh*
oil level	el nivel del aceite	*ehl neebehl deh ahtheyteh*
ointment	la pomada, el ungüento	*lah pohmahdah, ehl oongwehntoh*
ointment for burns	la pomada contra lasquemaduras	*lah pohmahdah kohntrah lahs kehmahdoorahs*
okay	vale, de acuerdo	*bahleh, deh ahkwehrdoh*
old	viejo	*byehhoh*
old part of town	el casco antiguo	*ehl kahskoh ahnteegwoh*
olive oil	el aceite de oliva	*ehl ahtheyteh deh ohleebah*
olives	las aceitunas	*lahs ahtheytoonahs*
omelette	la tortilla	*lah tohrteelyah*
on	sobre	*sohbreh*
on board	a bordo	*ah bohrdoh*
oncoming car	el vehículo que viene	*ehl beheekooloh keh byehneh*
one hundred grams	los cien gramos	*lohs thyehn grahmohs*
one-way traffic	la dirección única	*lah deerehkthyohn ooneekah*
onion	la cebolla	*lah thehbohlyah*
open (adj.)	abierto	*ahbyehrtoh*
open (verb)	abrir	*ahbreer*
opera	la ópera	*lah ohpehrah*
operate	operar	*ohpehrahr*
operator (telephone)	la operadora	*lah ohpehrahdohrah*
operetta	la opereta, la zarzuela	*lah ohpehrehtah, lah thahrthwehlah*
opposite	al frente, enfrente de	*ahl frehnteh, ehnfrehnteh deh*
optician	la óptica	*lah ohpteekah*
orange	la naranja	*lah nahrahnhah*
orange (adj.)	naranja	*nahrahnhah*
orange juice	el zumo de naranja	*ehl thoomoh deh nahrahnhah*
order (in -,) tidy	en orden, ordenado	*ehn ohrdehn, ohrdehnahdo*

order (verb)	pedir	*pehdeer*
order	el pedido	*ehl pehdeedoh*
other	otro	*ohtroh*
other side	el otro lado	*ehl ohtroh lahdoh*
outside	afuera	*ahfwehrah*
overtake	adelantar	*ahdehlahntahr*
oysters	las ostras	*lahs ohstrahs*

P

packed lunch	el paquete con bocadillos	*ehl pahkehteh kohn bohkahdeelyohs*
page	la página	*lah pahheenah*
pain	el dolor	*ehl dohlohr*
painkiller	el analgésico	*ehl ahnahlhehseekoh*
paint (verb)	pintar	*peentahr*
paint	la pintura	*lah peentoorah*
painting (art)	el cuadro	*ehl kwahdroh*
painting (object)	la pintura	*lah peentoorah*
palace	el palacio	*ehl pahlahthyoh*
pancake	la crepe	*lah krehp*
pane	el cristal	*ehl kreestahl*
pants (briefs)	las bragas	*lahs brahgahs*
panty liner	el protegeslip	*ehl prohtehhehsleep*
paper	el papel	*ehl pahpehl*
paraffin oil	el querosén	*ehl kehrohsehn*
parasol	el quitasol	*ehl keetahsohl*
parcel	el paquete	*ehl pahkehteh*
pardon	perdone	*pehrdohneh*
parents	los padres	*lohs pahdrehs*
park	el parque	*ehl pahrkeh*
park (verb)	aparcar	*ahpahrkahr*
parking space	el sitio para aparcar	*ehl seetyoh pahrah ahpahrkahr*
parsley	el perejil	*ehl pehrehheel*
partition	la secreción	*lah sehkrehthyohn*
partner	la pareja	*lah pahrehhah*

party	la fiesta	*lah fyehstah*
passable	practicable	*prahkteekahbleh*
passenger	el pasajero	*ehl pahsahhehroh*
passport	el pasaporte	*ehl pahsahpohrteh*
passport photo	la foto de carnet	*lah fohtoh deh kahrneh*
patient	el paciente	*ehl pahthyehnteh*
pavement	la acera	*lah ahthehrah*
pay (verb)	pagar	*pahgahr*
pay the bill	pagar la cuenta	*pahgahr lah kwehntah*
peach	el melocotón	*ehl mehlohkohtohn*
peanuts	los cacahuetes	*lohs kahkahwehtehs*
pear	la pera	*lah pehrah*
peas	los guisantes	*lohs gueesahntehs*
pedal	el pedal	*ehl pehdahl*
pedestrian crossing	el paso de peatones	*ehl pahsoh deh pehahtohnehs*
pedicure	la pedicura	*lah pehdeekoorah*
pen	la pluma	*lah ploomah*
pencil (hard/soft)	el lápiz (duro/blando)	*ehl lahpeeth (dooroh /blahndoh)*
penis	el pene	*ehl pehneh*
pepper (capsicum)	el pimiento	*ehl peemyehntoh*
pepper (condiment)	la pimienta	*lah peemyehntah*
performance	la función de teatro /música	*lah foonthyohn deh tehahtroh/mooseekah*
perfume	el perfume	*ehl pehrfoomeh*
perm (verb)	hacer una permanente	*ahthehr oonah pehrmahnehnteh*
perm	la permanente	*lah pehrmahnehnteh*
permit	el permiso	*ehl pehrmeesoh*
person	la persona	*lah pehrsohnah*
personal	personal	*pehrsohnahl*
petrol	la gasolina	*lah gahsohleenah*
petrol station	la gasolinera	*lah gahsohleenehrah*
pets	los animales domésticos	*lohs ahneemahles dohmehsteekohs*
pharmacy	la farmacia	*lah fahrmahthyah*

phone (by)	por teléfono	*pohr tehlehfohnoh* phone
(tele-)	el teléfono	*ehl tehlehfohnoh*
phone (verb)	llamar por teléfono	*lyahmahr pohr tehlehfohnoh*
phone box	la cabina telefónica	*lah kahbeenah tehlehfohneekah*
phone directory	la guía de teléfonos	*lah gheeah deh tehlehfohnohs*
phone number	el número de teléfono	*ehl noomehroh deh tehlehfohnoh*
photo	la foto	*lah fohtoh*
photocopier	la fotocopiadora	*lah fohtohkohpyahdohrah*
photocopy (verb)	fotocopiar	*fohtohkohpyahr*
photocopy	la fotocopia	*lah fohtohkohpyah*
pick up (fetch person)	(ir a) buscar, pasar a buscar	*(eer ah) booskahr, pahsahr ah booskahr*
picnic	el picnic	*ehl peekneek*
piece of clothing	la prenda	*lah prehndah*
pier	el muelle	*ehl mwehlyeh*
pigeon	la paloma	*lah pahlohmah*
pill (contraceptive)	la píldora (anticonceptiva)	*lah peeldohrah (ahnteekohnthehpteebah)*
pillow	la almohada	*lah ahlmohahdah*
pillowcase	la funda de almohada	*lah foondah deh ahlmohahdah*
pin	el alfiler	*ehl ahlfeelehr*
pineapple	la piña	*lah peenyah*
pipe	la pipa	*lah peepah*
pipe tobacco	el tabaco de pipa	*ehl tahbahkoh deh peepah*
pity	lástima	*lahsteemah*
place of entertainment	el sitio para salir	*ehl seetyoh pahrah sahleer*
place of interest	el punto de interés	*ehl poontoh deh eentehrehs*
plan/map	el plano	*ehl plahnoh*
plant	la planta	*lah plahntah*
plasters	las tiritas, los esparadrapos	*lahs teereetahs, lohs ehspahrahdrahpohs*
plastic	el plástico	*ehl plahsteekoh*
plastic bag	la bolsita	*lah bohlseetah*

plate	el plato	*ehl plahtoh*
platform	la vía, el andén	*lah beeah, ehl ahndehn*
play (theatre)	la obra de teatro	*lah ohbrah deh tehahtroh*
play (verb)	jugar	*hoogahr*
playground	el parque infantil	*ehl pahrkeh eenfahnteel*
playing cards	los naipes	*lohs naypehs*
pleasant	agradable	*ahgrahdahbleh*
please	por favor	*pohr fahbohr*
pleasure	el placer	*ehl plahthehr*
plum	la ciruela	*lah theerwehlah*
pocketknife	la navaja	*lah nahbahhah*
point (verb)	indicar	*eendeekahr*
poison	el veneno	*ehl behnehnoh*
police	la policía	*lah pohleetheeah*
police station	la comisaría	*la kohmeesahreeah*
policeman	el guardia	*ehl gwahrdyah*
pond	el estanque	*ehl ehstahnkeh*
pony	el poney	*ehl pohnehy*
pop concert	el concierto pop	*ehl kohnthyehrtoh pohp*
population	la población	*lah pohblahthyohn*
pork	la carne de cerdo	*lah kahrneh deh thehrdoh*
port wine	el oporto	*ehl ohpohrtoh*
porter	el portero	*ehl pohrtehroh*
post code	el código postal	*ehl cohdeegoh pohstahl*
post office	la oficina de Correos	*lah ohfeetheenah deh cohrrehohs*
postage	el franqueo	*ehl frahnkehoh*
postbox	el buzón	*ehl boothohn*
postcard	la (tarjeta) postal	*lah (tahrhehtah) pohstahl*
postman	el cartero	*ehl kahrtehroh*
potato	la patata	*lah pahtahtah*
poultry	las aves	*lahs ahbehs*
powdered milk	la leche en polvo	*lah lehcheh ehn pohlboh*
power point	la toma de corriente	*lah tohmah deh kohrryehnteh*
pram	el cochecito	*ehl kohchehtheetoh*
prawns	las gambas	*lahs gahmbahs*
precious	querido	*kehreedoh*

prefer	preferir	*prehfehreer*
preference	la preferencia	*lah prehfehrehnthyah*
pregnant	embarazada	*ehmbahrahthahdah*
present	presente	*prehsehnteh*
present (gift)	el regalo	*ehl rehgahloh*
press (verb)	apretar	*ahprehtahr*
pressure	la tensión	*lah tehnsyohn*
price	el precio	*ehl prehthyoh*
price list	la lista de precios	*lah leestah deh prehthyohs*
print (verb)	copiar	*kohpyahr*
print	la copia	*lah kohpyah*
probably	probablemente	*prohbahblehmehnteh*
problem	el problema	*ehl prohblehmah*
profession	la profesión	*lah prohfehsyohn*
programme	el programa	*ehl prohgrahmah*
pronounce	pronunciar	*prohnoonthyahr*
propane camping gas	el gas propano	*ehl gahs prohpahnoh*
pull	sacar	*sahkahr*
pull a muscle	distender un músculo	*deestehndehr oon mooskooloh*
pure	puro	*pooroh*
purple	violeta	*beeohlehta*
purse	el monedero	*ehl mohnehdehroh*
push	empujar	*ehmpoohahr*
puzzle	el rompecabezas	*ehl rohmpehkahbehthahs*
pyjamas	el pijama	*ehl peehahmah*

Q

quarter	la cuarta parte	*lah kwahrtah pahrteh*
quarter of an hour	el cuarto de hora	*ehl kwahrtoh deh ohrah*
queen	la reina	*lah reheenah*
question	la pregunta	*lah prehgoontah*
quick	rápido	*rahpeedoh*
quiet	tranquilo	*trahnkeeloh*

R

radio	la radio	*lah rahdyoh*
railways	los ferrocarriles	*lohs fehrrohkahrreelehs*
rain (verb)	llover	*lyohbehr*
rain	la lluvia	*lah lyoobyah*
raincoat	el impermeable	*ehl eempehrmehahbleh*
raisins	las uvas pasas	*lahs oobahs pahsahs*
rape	la violación	*lah beeohlahthyohn*
rapids	el rápido	*ehl rahpeedoh*
rash (skin)	la erupción cutánea	*lah ehroopthyohn kootahnehah*
raspberries	las frambuesas	*lahs frahmbwehsahs*
raw	crudo	*kroodoh*
raw ham	el jamón (serrano)	*ehl hahmohn sehrrahnoh*
raw vegetables	las verduras crudas	*lahs behrdoorahs kroodahs*
razor blades	las hojas de afeitar	*lahs ohahs deh ahfeheetahr*
read (verb)	leer	*lehehr*
ready	listo	*leestoh*
really	en realidad	*ehn rehahleedahdh*
receipt	el recibo	*ehl rehtheeboh*
recipe	la receta	*lah rehthehtah*
reclining chair	la tumbona	*lah toombohnah*
recommend	recomendar	*rehkohmehndahr*
rectangle	el rectángulo	*ehl rehktahngooloh*
red	rojo	*rohhoh*
red wine	el vino tinto	*ehl beenoh teentoh*
refrigerator	el refrigerador	*ehl rehfreehehrahdohr*
regards	recuerdos	*rehkwehrdohs*
region	la región	*lah rehhyohn*
registered	certificado	*thehrteefeekahdoh*
relatives	los parientes	*lohs pahryehntehs*
reliable	fiable/seguro	*fyahbleh/sehgooroh*
religion	la religión	*lah rehleehyohn*
rent out	alquilar	*ahlkeelahr*
repair (verb)	arreglar	*ahrrehglahr*
repairs	el arreglo	*ehl ahrrehgloh*

repeat	repetir	*rehpehteer*
report	el atestado	*ehl ahtehstahdoh*
resent	tomar a mal	*tohmahr ah mahl*
responsible	responsable	*rehspohnsahbleh*
rest (verb)	descansar	*dehskahnsahr*
restaurant	el restaurante	*ehl rehstahoorahnteh*
retired	jubilado	*hoobeeladoh*
retirement	la jubilación	*lah hoobeelahthyohn*
return (ticket)	el billete de ida y vuelta	*ehl beelyehteh deh eedah ee bwehltah*
reverse (vehicle)	dar marcha atrás	*dahr mahrchah ahtrahs*
rheumatism	el reuma	*ehl rehoomah*
rice	el arroz	*ehl ahrrohth*
ridiculous	tontería(s)	*tohntehreeah(s)*
riding (horseback)	montar a caballo	*mohntahr ah kahbahlyoh*
riding school	el picadero	*ehl peekahdehroh*
right	derecha	*dehrehchah*
right (on the)	a la derecha	*ah lah dehrehchah*
right of way	la preferencia	*lah prehfehrehnthyah*
ripe	maduro	*mahdooroh*
risk	el riesgo	*ehl ryehsgoh*
river	el río	*ehl reeoh*
road	el camino	*ehl kahmeenoh*
roadway	la calzada	*lah kahlthahdah*
roasted	asado	*ahsahdoh*
rock	la roca	*lah rohkah*
rolling tobacco	el tabaco para liar	*ehl tahbahkoh pahrah leeahr*
roof rack	la baca	*lah bahkah*
room	la habitación	*lah ahbeetahthyohn*
room number	el número de la habitación	*ehl noomehroh deh lah ahbeetahthyohn*
room service	el servicio en la habitación	*ehl sehrbeethyoh ehn lah ahbeetahthyohn*
rope	la cuerda	*lah kwehrdah*
rosé	el vino rosado	*ehl beenoh rohsahdoh*
roundabout	la rotonda	*lah rohtohndah*

route	la ruta	*lah rootah*
rowing boat	el bote de remos	*ehl bohteh deh rehmohs*
rubber	la goma	*lah gohmah*
rubbish	tontería(s)	*tohntehreeah(s)*
rucksack	la mochila	*lah mohcheelah*
rude	descortés/ maleducado	*dehskohrtehs/ mahlehdookahdoh*
ruins	las ruinas	*lahs rweenahs*
run into	encontrar	*ehnkohntrahr*

S

sad	triste	*treesteh*
safari	el safari	*ehl sahfahree*
safe	la caja fuerte	*lah kahhah fwehrteh*
safe/secure	seguro	*sehgooroh*
safety pin	el imperdible	*ehl eempehrdeebleh*
sail	la vela	*lah behlah*
sailing boat	el velero	*ehl behlehroh*
salad	la ensalada	*lah ehnsahlahdah*
salad oil	el aceite	*ehl ahthehyteh*
salami	el salami	*ehl sahlahmee*
sale	las rebajas, la liquidación	*lahs rehbahhahs, lah leekeedahthyohn*
salt	la sal	*lah sahl*
same	mismo	*meesmoh*
same	lo mismo	*loh meesmoh*
sandwich	el bocadillo	*ehl bohkahdeelyoh*
sandy beach	la playa de arena	*lah plahyah deh ahrehnah*
sanitary towel	la compresa	*lah kohmprehsah*
sardines	las sardinas	*lahs sahrdeenahs*
satisfied	contento	*kohntehntoh*
Saturday	el sábado	*ehl sahbahdoh*
sauce	la salsa	*lah sahlsah*
saucepan	la cacerola	*lah kahthehrohlah*
sauna	la sauna	*lah sahoonah*
sausage	el embutido	*ehl ehmbooteedoh*

savoury	salado	*sahlahdoh*
say (verb)	decir	*dehtheer*
scarf	la bufanda (woollen)	*lah boofahndah*
scarf	el pañuelo	*ehl pahnywehloh*
scenic walk	la visita a la ciudad (a pie)	*lah beeseetah ah lah thyoodahdh (ah pyeh)*
school	la escuela	*lah ehskwehlah*
scissors	las tijeras	*lahs teehehrahs*
scooter	la vespa	*lah behspah*
scrambled eggs	los huevos revueltos	*lohs wehbohs rehbwehltohs*
screw	el tornillo	*ehl tohrneelyoh*
screwdriver	el destornillador	*ehl dehstohrneelyahdohr*
sculpture	la escultura	*lah ehskooltoorah*
sea	el mar	*ehl mahr*
seasick	mareado	*mahrehahdoh*
seat	el asiento	*ehl ahsyehntoh*
seat	el asiento, la butaca	*ehl ahsyehntoh, lah bootahkah*
second (adj.)	segundo	*sehgoondoh*
second	el segundo	*ehl sehgoondoh*
second-hand	de segunda mano	*deh sehgoondah mahnoh*
sedative	el calmante	*ehl kahlmahnteh*
see (person)	visitar	*beeseetahr*
see	mirar	*meerahr*
self-timer	el disparador automático	*ehl deespahrahdohr ahootohmahteekoh*
semi-skimmed	semidesnatado	*sehmeedehsnahtahdoh*
send	enviar	*ehnbyahr*
sentence	la frase	*lah frahseh*
September	septiembre	*sehptyehmbreh*
serious	grave	*grahbeh*
service	el servicio	*ehl sehrbeethyoh*
serviette	la servilleta	*lah sehrbeelyehtah*
set (verb)	marcar	*mahrkahr*
sewing thread	el hilo de coser	*ehl eeloh deh kohsehr*
shade	la sombra	*lah sohmbrah*
shallow	poco profundo	*pohkoh prohfoondoh*

shampoo	el champú	*ehl chahmpoo*
shark	el tiburón	*ehl teeboorohn*
shave (verb)	afeitar	*ahfeheetahr*
shaver	la afeitadora eléctrica	*lah ahfehytahdohrah ehlehktreekah*
shaving brush	la brocha de afeitar	*lah brohchah deh ahfeheetahr*
shaving cream	la crema de afeitar	*lah krehmah deh ahfeheetahr*
shaving soap	el jabón de afeitar	*ehl hahbohn deh ahfeheetahr*
sheet	la sábana	*lah sahbahnah*
sherry	el jerez	*ehl hehrehth*
shirt	la camisa	*lah kahmeesah*
shoe	el zapato	*ehl thahpahtoh*
shoe polish	la crema de zapatos	*lah krehmah deh thahpahtohs*
shoe shop	la zapatería	*lah thahpahtehreeah*
shoelaces	los cordones	*lohs kohrdohnehs*
shoemaker	el zapatero	*ehl thahpahtehroh* shop
(verb)	hacer la compra	*ahthehr lah kohmprah*
shop	la tienda	*lah tyehndah*
shop assistant	la vendedora	*lah behndehdohrah*
shop window	el escaparate	*ehl ehskahpahrahteh*
shopping centre	el centro comercial	*ehl thehntroh kohmehrthyahl*
short	corto	*kohrtoh*
short circuit	el cortocircuito	*ehl kohrtohtheerkweetoh*
shoulder	el hombro	*ehl ohmbroh*
show	el espectáculo	*ehl ehspehktahkooloh*
shower	la ducha	*lah doochah*
shutter	el obturador	*ehl ohbtoorahdohr*
sieve	el tamiz	*ehl tahmeeth*
sign (verb)	firmar	*feermahr*
sign	el cartel	*ehl kahrtehl*
signature	la firma	*lah feermah*
signposted walk	la excursión señalizada	*lah ehxkooresyohn sehnyahleethahdah*

silence	el silencio	*ehl seelehnthyoh*
silver	la plata	*lah plahtah*
silver-plated	plateado	*plahtehahdoh*
simple	sencillo	*sehntheelyoh*
single (unmarried)	soltero	*sohltehroh*
single	individual	*eendeebeedwahl*
single ticket	el billete de ida	*ehl beelyehteh deh eedah*
sir	señor	*sehnyohr*
sister	la hermana	*lah ehrmahnah*
sit	estar sentado	*ehstahr sehntahdoh*
size (shoes)	el número	*ehl noomehroh*
size	la talla	*lah tahlyah*
ski boots	las botas de esquí	*lahs bohtahs deh ehskee*
ski goggles	las gafas de esquí	*lahs gahfahs deh ehskee*
ski instructor	el profesor de esquí	*ehl prohfehsohr deh ehskee*
ski lessons/class	la clase de esquiar	*lah klahseh deh ehskeeahr*
ski lift	el telesquí	*ehl tehlehskee*
ski pants	los pantalones de esquiar	*lohs pahntahlohnehs deh ehskeeahr*
ski pass	el bono (de remontes/esquí)	*ehl bohnoh (deh rehmohntehs/ehskee)*
ski slope	la pista de esquí (alpino)	*lah peestah deh ehskee (ahlpeenoh)*
ski stick	el bastón de esquí	*ehl bahstohn deh ehskee*
ski suit	el traje de esquiar	*ehl trahheh deh ehskeeahr*
ski wax	la cera para esquí	*lah thehrah pahrah ehskee*
ski/skiing	esquiar, el esquí	*ehskeeahr, ehl ehskee*
skin	la piel	*lah pyehl*
skirt	la falda	*lah fahldah*
skis	los esquís	*lohs ehskees*
sleep (verb)	dormir	*dohrmeer*
sleep well!	que descanse	*keh dehskahnseh*
sleeping car	el coche cama	*ehl kohcheh kahmah*
sleeping pills	los somníferos	*lohs sohmneefehrohs*
slide	la diapositiva	*lah deeahpohseeteebah*
slip (women's)	la combinación	*lah kohmbeenahthyohn*
slip road	la entrada	*lah ehntrahdah*

slow	despacio	*dehspahthyoh*
slow train	el tren ómnibus	*ehl trehn ohmneeboos*
small	pequeño	*pehkehnyoh*
small change	el cambio, el dinero suelto	*ehl kahmbyoh, ehl deenehroh swehltoh*
smell unpleasant (verb)	oler mal	*ohlehr mahl*
smoke	el humo	*ehl oomoh*
smoke (verb)	fumar	*foomahr*
smoked	ahumado	*ahoomahdoh*
smoking compartment	el departamento de fumadores	*ehl dehpahrtahmehntoh deh foomahdohrehs*
snake	la serpiente	*lah sehrpyehnteh*
snorkel	el esnórquel	*ehl ehsnohrkehl*
snow (verb)	nevar	*nehbahr*
snow	la nieve	*lah nyehbeh*
snow chains	la cadena antideslizante	*lah kahdehnah ahnteedehsleethahnte*
soap	el jabón	*ehl hahbohn*
soap box	la jabonera	*lah hahbohnehrah* soap
powder	el jabón en polvo	*ehl hahbohn ehn pohlboh*
soccer	el fútbol	*ehl footbohl*
soccer match	el partido de fútbol	*ehl pahrteedoh deh footbohl*
socket	el enchufe	*ehl ehnchoofeh*
socks	los calcetines	*lohs kahlthehteenehs*
soft drink	el refresco	*ehl rehfrehskoh*
sole (fish)	el lenguado	*ehl lehngwahdoh*
sole	la suela	*lah swehlah*
solicitor	el abogado	*ehl ahbohgahdoh*
someone	alguien	*ahlgyehn*
sometimes	a veces	*ah behthehs*
somewhere	en alguna parte	*ehn ahlgoonah pahrteh*
son	el hijo	*ehl eehoh*
soon	pronto	*prohntoh*
sorbet	el sorbete	*ehl sohrbehteh*
sore	la úlcera	*lah oolthehrah*
sore throat	el dolor de garganta	*ehl dohlohr deh gahrgahntah*
sorry	perdón	*pehrdohn*

sort/type	la clase	*lah klahseh*
soup	la sopa	*lah sohpah*
sour	agrio	*ahgreeoh*
sour cream	la nata ácida	*lah nahtah ahtheedah*
source	la fuente	*lah fwehnteh*
south	el sur	*ehl soor*
souvenir	el recuerdo de viaje	*ehl rehkwehrdoh deh byahheh*
spaghetti	los espaguetis	*lohs ehspahghehtees*
Spanish	español	*ehspahnyohl*
spanner (openended)	la llave (de boca)	*lah lyahbeh(deh bohkah)*
spanner	la llave de tuercas	*lah lyahbeh deh twehrkahs*
spare	la reserva	*lah rehsehrbah*
spare part	la pieza de recambio	*lah pyehthah deh rehkahmbyoh*
spare tyre	el neumático de reserva	*ehl nehoomahteekoh deh rehsehrbah*
spare wheel	la rueda de recambio	*lah rwehdah deh rehkahmbyoh*
speak	hablar	*ahblahr*
special	especial	*ehspehthyahl*
specialist	el especialista	*ehl ehspethyahleestah*
specialty	la especialidad	*lah ehspehthyahleedah*
speed limit	la velocidad máxima	*lah behlohtheedahdh mahxeemah*
spell (verb)	deletrear	*dehlehtrehahr*
spicy	picante	*peekahnteh*
splinter	la astilla	*lah ahsteelyah*
spoon	la cuchara	*lah koochahrah*
spoonful	la cucharada	*lah koochahrahdah*
sport (play)	hacer deporte	*ahthehr dehpohrteh*
sport	el deporte	*ehl dehpohrteh*
sports centre	la sala de deportes	*lah sahlah deh dehpohrtehs*
spot/place	el sitio	*ehl seetyoh*
sprain (verb)	torcerse	*tohrthehrseh*
spring	la primavera	*lah preemahbehrah*
square	el cuadrado	*ehl kwahdrahdoh*

square (town)	la plaza	*lah plahthah*
square metre(s)	metro(s) cuadrado(s)	*mehtroh(s) kwahdrahdoh(s)*
squash	el squash	*ehl skwahsh*
stadium	el estadio	*ehl ehstahdyoh*
stain	la mancha	*lah mahnchah*
stain remover	el quitamanchas	*ehl keetahmahnchahs*
stairs	las escaleras	*lahs ehskahlehrahs*
stalls (theatre)	la platea	*lah plahtehah*
stamp	el sello	*ehl sehlyoh*
start (car)	arrancar	*ahrrahnkahr*
station	la estación	*lah ehstahthyohn*
statue	la estatua	*lah ehstahtooah*
stay (lodge)	alojarse	*ahlohhahrseh*
stay (verb)	quedarse	*kehdahrseh*
stay	la estancia	*lah ehstahnthyah*
steal (verb)	robar	*rohbahr*
steel, stainless	el acero, inoxidable	*ehl ahthehroh, eenohxeedahbleh*
stench	el mal olor	*ehl mahl ohlohr*
sting (verb)	picar	*peekahr*
stitch (med.)	el punto	*ehl poontoh*
stitch (verb)	suturar	*sootoorahr*
stock	el caldo	*ehl kahldoh*
stockings	las medias	*lahs mehdyahs*
stomach	el estómago, el vientre	*ehl ehstohmahgoh, ehl byehntreh*
stomach ache	el dolor de vientre/ estómago	*ehl dohlohr deh byehntreh/ehstohmahgoh*
stomach cramps	los retortijones	*lohs rehtohrteehohnehs*
stools	las heces	*lahs ehthehs*
stop (verb)	parar	*pahrahr*
stop	la parada	*lah pahrahdah*
stopover	la escala	*lah ehskahlah*
storm	la tormenta	*lah tohrmehntah*
straight	liso	*leesoh*
straight ahead	todo recto	*tohdoh rehktoh*
straw	la pajita	*lah pahheetah*

strawberries	las fresas	*lahs frehsahs*
street	la calle	*lah kahlyeh*
street side	el lado de la calle	*ehl lahdoh deh lah kahlyeh*
strike	la huelga	*lah wehlgah*
strong (tobacco)	negro	*nehgroh*
study (verb)	estudiar	*ehstoodyahr*
stuffing	el relleno	*ehl rehlyehnoh*
subscriber's number	el número de abonado	*ehl noomehroh deh ahbohnahdoh*
subtitled	subtitulada	*soobteetoolahdah*
succeed	salir bien	*sahleer byehn*
sugar	el azúcar	*ehl ahthookahr*
sugar lumps	los terrones de azúcar	*lohs tehrrohnehs deh ahthookahr*
suit	el traje	*ehl trahheh*
suitcase	la maleta	*lah mahlehtah*
summer	el verano	*ehl behrahnoh*
summertime	la hora de verano	*lah ohrah deh behrahnoh*
sun	el sol	*ehl sohl*
sun hat	el sombrero de playa	*ehl sohmbrehroh deh plahyah*
sunbathe	tomar el sol	*tohmahr ehl sohl*
Sunday	el domingo	*ehl dohmeengoh*
sunglasses	las gafas de sol	*lahs gahfahs deh sohl*
sunrise	la salida del sol	*lah sahleedah dehl sohl*
sunset	la puesta del sol	*lah pwehstah dehl sohl*
sunstroke	la insolación	*lah eensohlahthyohn*
suntan lotion	la crema solar	*lah krehmah sohlahr*
suntan oil	el aceite bronceador	*ehl ahthehyteh brohnthehahdohr*
supermarket	el supermercado	*ehl soopehrmehrkahdoh*
surcharge	el suplemento	*ehl sooplehmehntoh*
surf	el surf	*ehl soorf*
surf board	la tabla de surf	*lah tahblah deh soorf*
surgery	la consulta	*lah kohnsooltah*
surname	el apellido	*ehl ahpehlyeedoh*
surprise	la sorpresa	*lah sohrprehsah*

swallow (verb)	tragar	*trahgahr*
swamp	el terreno pantanoso	*ehl tehrrehnoh pahntahnohsoh*
sweat	el sudor	*ehl soodohr*
sweet	el caramelo	*ehl kahrahmehloh*
sweet	dulce	*dooltheh*
sweetcorn	el maíz	*ehl maheeth*
sweetener	la sacarina	*lah sahkahreenah*
sweets	las golosinas	*lahs gohlohseenahs*
swim (verb)	nadar	*nahdahr*
swimming pool	la piscina	*lah peestheenah*
swimming trunks	el bañador	*ehl bahnyahdohr*
swindle	la estafa	*lah ehstahfah*
switch	el interruptor	*ehl eentehrrooptohr*
synagogue	la sinagoga	*lah seenahgohgah*

T

table	la mesa	*lah mehsah*
table tennis	el pingpong	*ehl peenpohn*
tablet	la tableta	*lah tahblehtah*
take (photograph)	sacar	*sahkahr*
take (time)	durar, tardar	*doorahr, tahrdahr*
take (verb)	emplear, usar, tomar	*ehmplehahr, oosahr, tohmahr*
take pictures	fotografiar, sacar fotos	*fohtohgrahfyahr, sahkahr fohtohs*
taken	ocupado	*ohkoopahdoh*
talcum powder	el talco	*ehl tahlkoh*
talk (verb)	hablar	*ahblahr*
tampons	los tampones	*lohs tahmpohnehs*
tap	el grifo	*ehl greefoh*
tap water	el agua del grifo	*ehl ahgwah dehl greefoh*
tart	la tarta	*lah tahrtah*
taste (verb)	probar	*prohbahr*
tax free shop	la tienda libre de impuestos	*lah tyehndah leebreh deh eempwehstohs*
taxi	el taxi	*ehl tahxee*

taxi stand	la parada de taxis	*lah pahrahdah deh tahxees*
tea	el té	*ehl teh*
teapot	la tetera	*lah tehtehrah*
teaspoon	la cuchara de té	*lah koochahrah deh teh*
telegram	el telegrama	*ehl tehlehgrahmah*telephoto
lens	el teleobjetivo	*ehl tehlehohbhehteeboh*
television	la televisión	*lah tehlehbeesyohn*
telex	el télex	*ehl tehlehx*
temperature	la temperatura	*lah tehmpehrahtoorah*
temporary filling	el empaste provisional	*ehl ehmpahsteh prohbeesyohnahl*
tender	tierno	*tyehrnoh*
tennis	el tenis	*ehl tehnees*
tennis ball	la pelota de tenis	*lah pehlohtah deh tehnees*
tennis court	la pista de tenis	*lah peestah deh tehnees*
tennis racket	la raqueta de tenis	*lah rahkehtah deh tehnees*
tennis shoes	los zapatos de tenis	*lohs thahpahtohs deh tehnees*
tenpin bowling	los bolos	*lohs bohlohs*
tent	la tienda	*lah tyehndah*
tent peg	la estaca	*lah ehstahkah*
terrace	la terraza	*lah tehrrahthah*
terrible	terrible	*tehrreebleh*
thank (verb)	agradecer	*ahgrahdehthehr*
thank you	gracias	*grahthyahs*
thaw	deshelar	*dehsehlahr*
the day after tomorrow	pasado mañana	*pahsahdoh mahnyahnah*
theatre	el teatro	*ehl tehahtroh*
theft	el robo	*ehl rohboh*
there	allí	*ahlyee*
thermal bath	el baño termal	*ehl bahnyoh tehrmahl*
thermometer	el termómetro	*ehl tehrmohmehtroh*
thick	grueso/gordo	*grwehsoh/gohrdoh*
thief	el ladrón	*ehl lahdrohn*
thigh	el muslo	*ehl moosloh*
thin	fino, flaco	*feenoh, flahkoh*
things	las cosas	*lahs kohsahs*

think	pensar	*pehnsahr*
third	la tercera parte	*lah tehrthehrah pahrteh*
thirsty, to be	la sed	*lah sehdh*
this afternoon	esta tarde	*ehstah tahrdeh*
this evening	esta noche	*ehstah nohcheh*
this morning	esta mañana	*ehstah mahnyahnah*
thread	el hilo	*ehl eeloh*
throat	la garganta	*lah gahrgahntah*
throat lozenges	las pastillas para la garganta	*lahs pahsteelyahs pahrah lah gahrgahntah*
throw up	vomitar	*bohmeetahr*
thunderstorm	la tormenta eléctrica	*lah tohrmehntah ehlehktreekah*
Thursday	el jueves	*ehl hwehbehs*
ticket (admission)	la entrada	*lah ehntrahdah*
ticket (travel)	el billete	*ehl beelyehteh*
tickets	los billetes	*lohs beelyehtehs*
tidy (verb)	recoger	*rehkohehr*
tie	la corbata	*lah kohrbahtah*
tights	el leotardo, el panty	*ehl lehohtahrdoh, ehl pahntee*
time (occasion)	la vez	*lah behth*
time	el tiempo	*ehl tyehmpoh*
timetable	el horario	*ehl ohrahryoh*
tip (money)	la propina	*lah prohpeenah*
tissues	los pañuelitos de papel	*lohs pahnywehleetohs de pahpehl*
toast	el pan tostado, las tostadas	*ehl pahn tohstahdoh, lahs tohstahdahs*
tobacco	el tabaco	*ehl tahbahkoh*
toboggan	el trineo	*ehl treenehoh*
today	hoy	*oy*
toe	el dedo del pie	*ehl dehdoh dehl pyeh*
together	juntos	*hoontohs*
toilet	el water/ los servicios/ el lavabo	*ehl bahtehr/lohs sehrbeethyohs, ehl lahbahboh*

toilet paper	el papel higiénico	*ehl pahpehl eehyehneekoh*
toiletries	los artículos de tocador	*lohs ahrteekoolohs deh tohkahdohr*
tomato	el tomate	*ehl tohmahteh*
tomato purée	el tomate triturado	*ehl tohmahteh treetoorahdoh*
tomato sauce	el ketchup	*ehl kehchoop*
tomorrow	mañana	*mahnyahnah*
tongue	la lengua	*lah lehngwah*
tonic water	el agua tónica	*ehl agwah tohneekah*
tonight	esta noche	*ehstah nohcheh*
too much	demasiado	*dehmahsyahdoh*
tools	las herramientas	*lahs ehrrahmyehntahs*
tooth	el diente	*ehl dyehnteh*
toothache	el dolor de muelas	*ehl dohlohr deh mwehlahs*
toothbrush	el cepillo de dientes	*ehl thehpeelyoh deh dyehntehs*
toothpaste	el dentífrico	*ehl dehnteefreekoh*
toothpick	el palillo	*ehl pahleelyoh*
top up	rellenar	*rehlyehnahr*
total	el total	*ehl tohtahl*
tough	duro	*dooroh*
tour	la excursión, el paseo	*lah ehxkoorsyohn, ehl pahsehoh*
tour guide	el guía	*ehl gheeah*
tourist card	la tarjeta de turista	*lah tahrhehtah deh tooreestah*
tourist class	la clase turista	*lah klahseh tooreestah*
Tourist Information office	la oficina de (información y) turismo	*lah ohfeetheenah deh (eenfohrmahthyohn ee) tooreesmoh*
tourist menu	el menú turístico	*ehl mehnoo tooreesteekoh*
tow	remolcar	*rehmohlkahr*
tow cable	el cable de remolque	*ehl kahbleh deh rehmohlkeh*
towel	la toalla	*lah tohahlyah*
tower	la torre	*lah tohrreh*
town hall	el ayuntamiento	*ehl ahyoontahmyehntoh*
town/city	la ciudad	*lah thyoodahdh*

toys	los juguetes	*lohs hoogehtehs*
traffic	el tráfico	*ehl trahfeekoh*
traffic light	el semáforo	*ehl sehmahfohroh* trailer
tent	el remolque tienda	*ehl rehmohlkeh tyehndah*
train	el tren	*ehl trehn*
train ticket	el billete de tren	*ehl beelyehteh deh trehn*
train timetable	la guía de trenes	*lah gueeah deh trehnehs*
translate	traducir	*trahdootheer*
travel (verb)	viajar	*byahhahr*
travel agent	la agencia de viajes	*lah ahhehnthyah deh byahhehs*
travel guide	la guía	*lah gheeah*
traveller	el pasajero	*ehl pahsahhehroh* traveller's
cheque	el cheque de viajero	*ehl chehkeh deh byahhehroh*
treacle/syrup	la melaza	*lah mehlahthah*
treatment	el tratamiento	*ehl trahtahmyehntoh*
triangle	el triángulo	*ehl treeahngooloh*
trim	cortar las puntas	*kohrtahr lahs poontahs*
trip	el paseo, la excursión	*ehl pahsehoh,lah ehxkoorsyohn*
trouble	la molestia	*lah mohlehstyah*
trousers (long, short)	los pantalones (cortos, largos)	*lohs pahntahlohnehs (kohrtohs,lahrgohs)*
trout	la trucha	*lah troochah*
trunk call	interurbano	*eentehroorbahnoh* trunk
code	el prefijo	*ehl prehfeehoh*
trustworthy	digno de confianza	*deegnoh deh kohnfyahnthah*
try on (clothes)	probarse	*prohbahrseh*
T-shirt	la camiseta	*lah kahmeesehtah*
tube	el tubo	*ehl tooboh*
Tuesday	el martes	*ehl mahrtehs*
tumble drier	la secadora	*lah sehkahdohrah*
tuna	el atún	*ehl ahtoon*
tunnel	el túnel	*ehl toonehl*
turn	la vez	*lah behth*
TV	la televisión	*lah tehlehbeesyohn*

tv and radio guide	la guía de radio y televisión	*lah gheeah deh rahdyoh ee tehlehbeesyohn*
tweezers	los alicates	*lohs ahleekahtehs* tyre
(bicycle)	la cubierta	*lah koobyehrtah*
tyre lever	el desmontador de neumáticos	*ehl dehsmohntahdohr deh nehoomahteekohs*
tyre pressure	la presión de los neumáticos	*lah prehsyohn deh lohs nehoomahteekohs*

U

ugly	feo	*fehoh*
umbrella	el paraguas	*ehl pahrahgwahs*
under	abajo, debajo de	*ahbahhoh, dehbahhoh deh*
underground railway	el metro	*ehl mehtroh*
underground railway system	la red de metro	*lah rehdh deh mehtroh*
underground station	la estación de metro	*lah ehstahthyohn deh mehtroh*
underpants	los calzoncillos	*lohs kahlthohntheelyohs*
understand	entender	*ehntehndehr*
underwear	la ropa interior	*lah rohpah eentehryohr*
undress (verb)	desvestirse	*dehsbehsteerseh*
unemployed	en paro	*ehn pahroh*
uneven	desigual	*dehseegwahl*
university	la universidad	*lah ooneebehrseedah*
unleaded	sin plomo	*seen plohmoh*
urgent	urgente	*oorhehnteh*
urine	la orina	*lah ohreenah*
usually	por lo general	*pohr loh hehnehrahl*

V

vacate	desalojar	*dehsahlohhahr*
vaccinate	vacunarse	*bahkoonahrseh*
vagina	la vagina	*lah bahheenah*
vaginal infection	la infección vaginal	*lah eenfehkthyohn bahheenal*

valid	válido	*bahleedoh*
valley	el valle	*ehl bahlyeh*
valuable	costoso	*kohstohsoh*
van	la furgoneta	*lah foorgohnehtah*
vanilla	la vainilla	*lah baheeneelyah*
vase	el florero	*ehl flohrehroh*
vaseline	la vaselina	*lah bahsehleenah*
veal	la carne de ternera	*lah kahrneh deh tehrnehrah*
vegetable soup	la sopa de verduras	*lah sohpah deh behrdoorahs*
vegetables	la verdura	*lah behrdoorah*
vegetarian	vegetariano	*behhehtahryahnoh*
vein	la vena	*lah vehnah*
vending machine	la máquina automática	*lah mahkeenah ahootohmahteekah*
venereal disease	la enfermedad venérea	*lah ehnfehrmehdahdh behnehrehah*
via	pasando por	*pahsahndoh pohr*
video recorder	el video	*ehl beedehoh*
video tape	la cinta de vídeo	*lah theentah deh beedehoh*
view	la vista	*lah beestah*
village	el pueblo	*ehl pwehbloh*
visa	el visado	*ehl beesahdoh*
visit (verb)	visitar	*beeseetahr*
visit	la visita	*lah beeseetah*
vitamin tablets	las tabletas de vitaminas	*lahs tahblehtahs deh beetahmeenahs*
vitamins	la vitamina	*lah beetahmeenah*
volcano	el volcán	*ehl bohlkahn*
volleyball (play)	jugar al vóleibol	*hoogahr ahl bohleheebohl*
vomit (verb)	vomitar	*bohmeetahr*

W

wait (verb)	esperar	*ehspehrahr*
waiter	el camarero	*ehl kahmahrehroh* waiting
room	la sala de espera	*lah sahlah deh ehspehrah*
waitress	la camarera	*lah kahmahrehrah* wake up

(verb)	despertar	*dehspehrtahr*
walk	el paseo	*ehl pahsehoh*
walk (take a)	salir a caminar	*sahleer ah kahmeenahr*
walk (verb)	ir (andando)	*eer(ahndahndoh)*
wallet	la cartera	*lah kahrtehrah*
wardrobe	el guardarropa	*ehl gwahrdahrrohpah*
warm	caliente	*kahlyehnteh*
warn	avisar, llamar	*ahbeesahr,lyahmahr*
warning	el aviso	*ehl ahbeesoh*
wash (verb)	lavar	*lahbahr*
washing (dirty)	la ropa sucia	*lah rohpah soothyah*
washing line	la cuerda de colgar la ropa	*lah kwehrdah deh kohlgahr lah rohpah*
washing machine	la lavadora	*lah lahbahdohrah*
washing-powder	el detergente	*ehl dehtehrhehnteh*
wasp	la avispa	*lah ahbeespah*
watch	el reloj	*ehl rehlohh*
water	el agua	*ehl ahgwah*
water ski	el esquí acuático	*ehl ehskee ahkwahteekoh*
waterproof	impermeable	*eempehrmehahbleh*
wave-pool	la piscina con oleaje	*lah peestheenah kohn ohlehahheh*
way (means)	el remedio	*ehl rehmehdyoh*
way (on the)	en el camino	*ehn ehl kahmeenoh*
way	el lado	*ehl lahdoh*
we	nosotros	*nohsohtrohs*
weak	débil	*dehbeel*
weather	el tiempo	*ehl tyehmpoh*
weather forecast	el pronóstico del tiempo	*ehl prohnohsteekoh dehl tyehmpoh*
wedding	la boda	*lah bohdah*
Wednesday	el miércoles	*ehl myehrkohlehs*
week	la semana	*lah sehmahnah*
weekend	el fin de semana	*ehl feen deh sehmahnah*
weekend duty	la guardia de fin de semana	*lah gwahrdyah deh feen deh sehmahnah*
weekly ticket	el abono semanal	*ehl ahbohnoh sehmahnahl*

welcome	bienvenido	*byehnbehneedoh*
well	bien, bueno	*byehn, bwehnoh*
west	el oeste	*ehl ohehsteh*
wet	mojado	*mohahdoh*
wet (weather)	lluvioso	*lyoobyohsoh*
wetsuit	el traje de surf	*ehl trahheh deh soorf*
what?	¿qué?	*keh?*
wheel	la rueda	*lah rwehdah*
wheelchair	la silla de ruedas	*lah seelyah deh rwehdahs*
when?	¿cuándo?	*kwahndoh?*
where?	¿dónde?	*dohndeh?*
which?	¿cuál?	*kwahl?*
whipped cream	el chantilly	*ehl chahnteelyee*
whipping cream	la nata para batir	*lah nahtah pahrah bahteer*
white	blanco	*blahnkoh*
who?	¿quién?	*kyehn?*
wholemeal	integral	*eentehgrahl*
wholemeal bread	el pan integral	*ehl pahn eentehgrahl*
why?	¿por qué?	*pohr keh?*
wide-angle lens	el objetivo gran angular	*ehl obhehteeboh grahn ahngoolahr*
widow	la viuda	*lah byoodah*
widower	el viudo	*ehl byoodoh*
wife	la mujer	*lah moohehr*
wind	el viento	*ehl byehntoh*
windbreak	la protección contra el viento	*lah prohtehkthyohn kohntrah ehl byehntoh*
windmill	el molino	*ehl mohleenoh*
window	la ventanilla, la ventana	*lah behntahneelyah, lah behntahnah*
windscreen wiper	el limpiaparabrisas	*ehl leempyahpahrahbreesahs*
wine	el vino	*ehl beenoh*
wine list	la carta de vinos	*lah kahrtah deh beenohs*
winter	el invierno	*ehl eenbyehrnoh*
witness	el testigo	*ehl tehsteegoh*
woman	la mujer	*lah moohehr*
wood	la madera	*lah mahdehrah*

wool	la lana	*lah lahnah*
word	la palabra	*lah pahlahbrah*
work	el trabajo	*ehl trahbahhoh*
working day	el día laborable	*ehl deeah lahbohrahbleh*
worn/used	gastado	*gahstahdoh*
worried	inquieto	*eenkyehtoh*
wound	la herida	*lah ehreedah*
wrap (verb)	envolver	*ehnbohlbehr*
wrist	la muñeca	*lah moonyehkah*
write	escribir	*ehskreebeer*
write down	apuntar	*ahpoontahr*
writing pad	el bloc (cuadriculado, a rayas)	*ehl blohk(kwahdreekoolahdoh, ah rahyahs)*
writing paper	el papel de escribir	*ehl pahpehl deh ehskreebeer*
written	por carta	*pohr kahrtah*
wrong	mal, equivocado	*mahl, ehkeebohkahdoh*

Y

yacht	el yate	*ehl yahteh*
year	el año	*ehl anyoh*
yellow	amarillo	*ahmahreelyoh*
yes	sí	*see*
yes, please	con (mucho) gusto	*kohn (moochoh) goostoh*
yesterday	ayer	*ahyehr*
yoghurt	el yogur	*ehl yohgoor*
you (formal)	usted	*oostehdh*
you too	igualmente	*eegwahlmehnteh*
youth hostel	el albergue juvenil	*ehl ahlbehrgeh hoobehneel*

Z

zip	la cremallera	*lah krehmahlyehrah*
zoo	el parque zoológico	*ehl pahrkeh thohohlohheekoh*

1 The article

Spanish nouns and adjectives are divided into 2 categories: masculine and feminine. The definite article (the) is **el** or **la**. Most masculine words end in **o** and most feminine words end in **a**.

el is used before masculine nouns, as in **el tren** (the train)
la is used before feminine nouns, as in **la playa** (the beach)
el is also used before feminine nouns beginning with a vowel, as in **el agua** (water).

Other examples are:

el techo	the roof	**la casa**	the house
el hambre	hunger	**el alma**	the soul

The plural of **el** is **los**; the plural of **la** is **las**.

In the case of the indefinite article (**a**, **an**):
un is used before masculine nouns, as in **un libro** (a book).
una is used before feminine nouns, as in **una mesa** (a table).
The plural is constructed by adding s, as in **unos camiones** (some lorries), **unas tazas** (some cups).

Other examples are:

un padre	a father	**una madre**	a mother
un hombre	a man	**una mujer**	a woman
unos hombres	men	**unas mujeres**	women

2 The plural

The plural of Spanish nouns and adjectives ends in **s**. Examples are:

singular	plural
el avión (the plane)	**los aviones**
la manzana (the apple)	**las manzanas**

3 Personal pronouns

I	**yo**
You	**tú/Usted**
He/she/it	**él/ella**
We	**nosotros/nosotras**
You	**vosotros/vosotras/Ustedes**
They	**ellos/ellas**

When speaking to a person one does not know well, Usted is used with the third person of the verb:
e.g. **Usted sabe/Ustedes saben** you know

4 Possessive pronouns

	masculine/feminine	plural
my	**mi**	**mis**
your	**tu**	**tus**
his/her/its	**su**	**sus**
our	**nuestro/nuestra**	**nuestros/nuestras**
your	**vuestro/vuestra**	**vuestros/vuestras**
their	**su**	**sus**

They agree with the object they modify, e.g. our car = **nuestro coche**.

5 Verbs

Note: pronouns are only used with verbs when absolutely necessary.

hablar	to speak
hablo	I speak
hablas	you speak
habla	he/she/you speak
hablamos	we speak
habláis	you speak
hablan	they/you speak

Here are some useful verbs:

ser	**estar** (to be)
soy	**estoy**
eres	**estás**
es	**está**
somos	**estamos**
sois	**estáis**
son	**están**

Note: **estar** is used with places and also means a temporary state, e.g. **el hotel está en la plaza**, (the hotel is in the square), **la niña está cansada** (the little girl is tired).

tener (to have)	**hacer** (to do/make)
tengo	**hago**
tienes	**haces**
tiene	**hace**
tenemos	**hacemos**
tenéis	**hacéis**
tienen	**hacen**

ir (to go)	**ver** (to see)
voy	**veo**
vas	**ves**
va	**ve**
vamos	**vemos**
vais	**veis**
van	**ven**

Negatives are formed by putting no before the verb:
e.g. **no entiendo**, I do not understand; **no oigo**, I cannot hear.

6 Basic prepositions

a = to, e.g. **voy a Madrid, voy al mercado.**
en= in or at, e.g. **estoy en la tienda, estoy en casa.**